Presented To:

From:

Date:

Truth Seekers

Truth Seekers

Ten Amazing People Who Found It

SID ROTH & MIKE SHREVE

DESTINY IMAGE. PUBLISHERS, INC.

P.O. Box 310, Shippensburg, PA 17257-0310

"Speaking to the Purposes of God for This Generation and for the Generations to Come."

This book and all other Destiny Image, Revival Press, MercyPlace, Fresh Bread, Destiny Image Fiction, and Treasure House books are available at Christian bookstores and distributors worldwide.

For a U.S. bookstore nearest you, call 1-800-722-6774.

For more information on foreign distributors, call 717-532-3040.

Reach us on the Internet: www.destinyimage.com.

ISBN 13 TP: 978-0-7684-3800-0

ISBN 13 Ebook: 978-0-7684-8989-7

ISBN 13 VTE: 978-0-7684-3865-9

For Worldwide Distribution, Printed in the U.S.A.

1 2 3 4 5 6 7 8 9 10 11 / 13 12 11

Dedication

To seekers of truth everywhere

Contents

Foreword

Recently, my good friend, Sid Roth, contacted me with a brilliant idea. He asked me to help put a book together highlighting the stories of ten truth seekers—where they came from, what they experienced on their journey and how they finally arrived at their goal.

I immediately felt a "surge" of enthusiasm (a word that appropriately means "*God within*"). Nothing could be closer to my heart. Even though I prayed about it overnight, I knew what my answer would be the next day, "Yes, I'd love to." And the project was launched.

Why was I invited to participate? I suppose the big factor was my background. Back in 1970, at the age of 19, I dropped everything—college, career hopes, money, relationships—to search for Ultimate Reality. I left college to study Kundalini Yoga under a guru named Yogi Bhajan. Later I taught that same yogic discipline at four universities and formed a yoga ashram in Tampa, Florida. (You can read my story in Chapter 7.) So yes, I've been down the road that many truth seekers take... and I'm familiar with all the twists, turns, hills, bumps, shady spots, bridges and ditches.

Why did I turn to Eastern religions and New Age thought? Probably, because I was disenchanted with traditional Christianity and its predictable rituals and sit-stand-kneel, church bulletin choreography. Furthermore, the exclusiveness bothered me immensely—the towering-church-steeple attitude, "My way is the right way and your way is the wrong way." I just couldn't align myself with that anymore. I sincerely felt it was a mindset from the Dark Ages. Breaking out of the preset religious mold seemed to be the only option, and exploring other religions and expressions of spirituality, the logical choice.

Besides, my amazing era witnessed some huge paradigm shifts resulting from brave free thinkers—like Martin Luther King Jr., who launched the Civil Rights Movement, and Mahatma Gandhi, who brought liberation to India through nonviolent means. "All You Need is Love" was the Beatles-inspired chant of the 1960s and 1970s. A tsunami-sized wave of change was crashing over the nations—powered, not by a "divide and conquer" attitude, but by a "unite and assimilate" philosophy. "Equality" was working politically and socially; it was only logical that this kind of mindset would overflow into realm of religion also.

But can you build some kind of "spiritual utopia" by branding all views of God and religion as equally legitimate and acceptable? Is that even logical? Is truth so "soupy" that it will conform to the shape of any "bowl"—or is truth a rock that doesn't change for anything or anyone?

This generation has witnessed remarkable scientific achievements, but how did we arrive at such superior knowledge? Certainly, we didn't get there by accepting every idea as legitimate, but by subjecting concepts and theories to experimentation and analysis, until the actual nature of a thing is discovered with absolute certainty (or close to it). "May the best opinion win!" What's wrong with that approach? Is it juvenile to think that way, or egotistical, or harsh, or hateful? No, of course not! That's the wise and mature way we do science; and the way we should do religion and spirituality as well.

If absolutes can be determined in the natural world (through science), can absolutes be determined in the spiritual world (through deductive reasoning and experiential knowledge)? Of course, they can! In every portion of the universe, from the natural cosmos to the heavenly realms, there is a divine order governed by laws.

Consider for a moment a major controversy during the first millennium A.D. and into the second. The BIG question in many people's minds concerned the nature of the solar system. "Does the sun revolve around the earth or the earth around the sun?"

There were respected thinkers on both sides of the table. Ptolemy, a second-century astronomer, taught that the sun revolved around the earth on a backdrop of unmoving stars. Everyone (well, almost everyone) bought into it—even the religious crowd growled "heretic!" if you dared to believe otherwise. Then about a thousand years later, at the peril of losing his life, Copernicus stirred the coals of controversy, insisting that the solar system was heliocentric (sun-centered). Did he rock the boat or what?

What if these two men had been contemporaries? What if they could have met each other? Would it be even remotely logical for Ptolemy and Copernicus to discuss their views and agree between themselves, "Truth is subjective. Copernicus, you have YOUR TRUTH and I, Ptolemy, can have MY TRUTH, and we can both be right simultaneously. Both of us can just CREATE our own reality."

To even imagine such a conversation not only "borders on the absurd," it crosses the boundary line altogether. One view *had* to be right at the expense of the other being wrong. Truth is objective; it's the same for all. Ironically, the popular, culturally "correct" view in Ptolemy's day was actually incorrect. "Hindsight" reveals the obvious now, but when it was fresh "insight," it wasn't so easy for people to accept. Revelations of truth can still be matters of controversy.

Was Copernicus unloving because he passionately upheld what he knew to be right? No. Would it have been better to sacrifice truth on an altar in order for the opposing parties to achieve unity with each other? No. Were Ptolemy and Copernicus "enemies" because they differed in their opinion? No, of course not!

And so it is spiritually. We are all searching for meaning in life. We are all pilgrims on a journey through time. We all tend to gaze upward and feel deeply that there's "something out there," eternal in nature, that is so much more important and fulfilling than mundane existence. Some pilgrims are more desperate than others to find the roadmap to eternity. The fact that you are reading this book leads me to believe you are a person of such spiritual caliber. You are on a quest and you are willing to explore the paths others have taken.

If we (the ten people featured in this book) express different views than the ones you presently embrace—please don't stop reading. Be slow to make final decisions. Open your heart. Entertain fresh ideas. Ask God's counsel. He will help you. He is quite involved in your journey... and He really wants you to know Him.

Finally... please realize that LOVE is our root motive. We truly LOVE YOU and want God's best for your life—now and forevermore.

In prayers for you,
Mike Shreve

Introduction

When I was in college, I started writing lyrics for songs and producing records. Shortly after graduating, I wrote a song that expressed the cry of my heart.

Although I had no debts, great health, a college degree, a wonderful wife, and a great job with an amazing future, something was missing. The song was titled, "There Must Be Something More!" The first words were, "Because I work, eat, sleep and that's the way it goes, there must be something more!" And the word *must* was almost a cry of desperation.

I was unsure what the solution might be. I just knew I was unhappy and went searching for happiness. But it's a big world out there—especially if you don't know what you're looking for. This started my search from gypsy to guru to fortuneteller to psychic. Nothing satisfied until I had an experience with the manifest presence of the love of God.

During the encounter, His light transformed every cell of my body. He touched me physically, spiritually, and emotionally. In His presence it was impossible to worry. No sickness, hurt, pain, or depression could coexist in this encounter.

Today, over 35 years later, I can say I have found that *something more*. God's tangible presence and peace never leave me. I literally am

directed by His voice in every area of my life. He supernaturally pro-
vides for every need in my life.

When I was on my journey, looking for happiness, I witnessed
power and miracles. I had good and bad experiences with the New
Age. But I have learned the good New Age experiences were anemic
compared to the love of God.

Now, through the real and incomparable power of the Spirit of
God, I have seen the blind regain sight, the deaf hear, the lame walk,
and the dead come back to life. More importantly, I have found the
only thing that can truly fill the emptiness in my heart that I felt so
many years ago.

I know as you read more about my life and the lives of the nine
other amazing truth seekers, your journey will be greatly enriched.

I believe you, too, are on a destiny path to experience the tangible,
rich, weighty love of God.

Shalom and Love,
Sid Roth

Chapter 1

From Hollywood to Heaven

By Robin Harfouche

*A rising star with psychic powers is paralyzed,
then receives a miracle from God!*

The log cabin was damp and cold. It was twilight, and the rising moon spilled silver streaks into the darkness of the cabin. I could barely make out the stark furnishings of the room: two roughly hewn chairs, a table, and the creaky iron bed I'd just left.

How did I get here? I wondered, walking toward the open window. Thick woods surrounded the cabin. A sense of foreboding clutched at my chest.

Suddenly, I saw a woman on horseback galloping toward me down a narrow path. I stood transfixed. She was wearing a long, dark, blue dress. On her feet were shiny black riding boots. A dark, hooded cloak flapped wildly as she drew nearer on her white steed. Her piercing, steel-blue eyes glared at me, beckoning me against my will.

"What do you want with me?" I screamed. Unseen hands pushed me from behind toward the door, which now swung open by itself. "No!" I cried, trying to resist. The woman dismounted, heading straight for me. "No! No! No!" I screamed, my strength waning.

My eyes flew open. No woman. No unseen hands. Only darkness and the thumping of my own heart. A chilly California breeze played with the yellow curtains framing my bedroom window. Trembling, I murmured, *"Our Father, which art in heaven, hallowed by Thy name…"* I couldn't remember where I learned the words—certainly not in church, for my family never went—but they always comforted me. Somewhere between darkness and dawn I finally fell asleep, trying to convince myself, "It was only a dream…"

When I told the recurring dream to my mother, she said, "That sounds exactly like my grandmother." Her voice trembled, "When I was a little girl, she used to scare me to death. She was a witch." I must have blanched pale as a ghost, because Mom quickly added, "But don't worry, honey. She's dead now."

And so began my initiation into the spiritual warfare that raged for generations over my family, a war between good and evil. On one side were black, satanic witches—on the other, Spirit-filled believers.

The black witches believed someone in just about every generation would be born with what they called "the veil," a supernatural "gift" of ESP—extrasensory perception. I was the one. From a young age I'd been able to read people's minds. I saw things and felt things no one else seemed to perceive.

My Grandparents Ranch

As a result, I was considered a super-sensitive kid. Because of this, I was an open target for the bullies in my school and neighborhood. It was so bad, after kindergarten was over, my parents decided

18

to send me to my grandparents' prune ranch for the summer, about 45 minutes away. I was ecstatic; Grandpa and Grandma were wonderful. Unknown to me, a visit that was only supposed to last for three months would stretch into years.

The ranch house was surrounded by three green hills, and in front of the house stood the big brown barn. When we arrived, Grandpa confided, "I've got a surprise waitin' for you." He led me to one of the stalls in the barn. There she was—a young Holstein-Friesan calf. I stroked her soft fur and immediately dubbed her "Clara." We became the best of friends.

The long summer days passed quickly as I threw myself into ranch life—helping Grandpa with chores, picking apples for Grandma's pies, and talking to the animals, who seemed to understand me better than people. Sometimes I took Clara to a huge alfalfa field near the ranch, where she would graze contentedly for hours while I strung wildflower necklaces for her.

Then it happened—an intrusion that brought pain and confusion swirling like dark storm clouds into my mind and life. Grandpa hired James, a 20-year-old neighbor with greasy black hair and an acne-scarred complexion, to help him with some fence-work. Eventually they asked him to babysit me once a month, on the recurring Friday night when both Grandpa and Grandma had to be gone.

James crept into my bedroom that first night under the guise of "tucking me in," but his intentions were altogether different. He threatened to kill me if I ever told. I was robbed of my innocence. Eventually, it escalated to "going all the way." During those monthly "nights of horror" I learned to simply lie still, pretend I was asleep, and endure it. Squeezing my eyes shut, I would imagine myself inside a little black box in my mind where he couldn't "touch" me. Once inside this box, I started hearing voices.

"Come up here with us!" the chorus of voices would say gleefully. "He can't get you here." Eager to join these beckoning new friends, I would rise above my bed. I could see my physical self still in bed, but my real self would ascend until I was traveling in space, surrounded by stars. One special place I went to was full of children—at least, I thought they were children. "You're special," they would tell me. "You're not like other people."

After James finished and retreated to another part of the house, I would see myself coming back toward the earth—then I would be back in bed, inside my body again. A gold shimmery thread connected me to my body, and the "children" told me never to let go of it. It was my connection. I somehow knew that if I lost that, I would lose myself.

By the time I was 12 I figured out James really wasn't going to kill me if I talked, but now shame kept me silent. One day, I found the courage to call Mom and tell her I wanted to come home. She wondered at the urgency in my voice, but she and Dad came to pick me up the very next day, no questions asked. I was glad to be home again.

I didn't realize how traumatized I was. I just knew I'd been violated by an adult that was supposed to care for me and protect me. To counteract that "victim" mentality, I became an overachiever. I thought if I could get a 4.0 average, be listed in *Who's Who*, and become the best at whatever I did, people would love me. At the age 15, I was an honor student, homecoming queen, head cheerleader, head majorette, Miss Solano County, and voted by my classmates as "Most Likely to Succeed."

Everything seemed to be going so much better, but then, the "other realm" made another play for my soul. Before my junior year, I was selected to travel to England with a group of students. It was there that I had my first taste of how frighteningly real the psychic realm can be.

A Shakespearean Drama

We landed at Heathrow Airport, then made the trip out to Kings College where we were staying. I was staring out the window of my room, gazing at the ancient cobblestone pathways. Just the day before, as the bus sloshed through the streets of London, I felt something strange come over me—an indefinable weakness permeating my body. Probably jet lag, I told myself. But this morning I couldn't shake off the feeling.

Firm rapping at the door brought me out of my reverie. "Coming!" I shouted. It was Katrina, a girl I'd met on the flight from California. Only 16, she seemed to possess an adult-like authority that was unnerving—intriguing. Her father was one of the trip counselors.

As we were leaving for our bus ride to Shakespeare's birthplace, she slipped something into her jacket pocket. "What's that?" I asked. "Just my tarot cards," she said, "I'll show them to you later." When we arrived, I suggested, "Why don't we start with Anne Hathaway's cottage."

We strolled through the manicured garden leading to the entrance of the cottage, then stepped inside. Cool, dank air and the stillness of centuries enclosed us. Fascinated with history, I soon found myself alone on the second floor. My attention was drawn to two gilded books with green leather bindings that lay open on the desk.

As I leaned down to read the ancient print, suddenly, like a camera zooming in, my eyes riveted on a single word written on the page. It was my name. No! This can't be, I thought, my chest tightening. ROBIN. ROBIN. ROBIN. The sound of my name echoed in my head. Terrified, I bumped into the wall. Wincing, I looked down the staircase. What I saw didn't make sense. A little girl in a long, white nightgown was falling backward down the steep incline. "Help me! Help me!" she screamed, her arms outstretched, her eyes pleading. I watched in horror as she landed with a thud, lifeless. I started sobbing. I'd just witnessed the death of a child.

Someone grabbed me around the waist. I gasped. It was only Katrina. As we walked to a bench in the garden, she whispered, "I see what you see."

"You what?"

"I see the little girl. I see the long, white nightgown. I see her falling downstairs."

Her father, Mr. Holmes, patted my shoulder, saying, "It's all right, Robin. This area is full of spiritual presences."

When I told him what I saw, his only explanation was, "You probably lived here in another life. Perhaps that little girl was you."

It was all too strange. On the ride back, Mr. Holmes talked candidly of the psychic realm. It was from him I first learned the term *New Age*.

That night, I slept fitfully, troubled by disturbing dreams. Suddenly a loud THWACK! jolted me awake. The double, hinged window across the room had opened and was banging against the wall. I knew something was in my room. I rushed over to Katrina's room. "You can't let these spirits control you," she said matter-of-factly. I grabbed my pillow and quilt and made a pallet on the floor beside Katrina's bed, sleeping soundly the rest of the night. The next morning she taught me how to use tarot cards. Three weeks later we flew back to California. I never saw Katrina again—but her influence remained.

The Spiritual Stalker

September of 1975, I enrolled at California Polytechnic State University. Little did I know I would meet a "stalker" there ... from another realm. One day, on my way to class, I heard a loud whistle behind me. I turned around, but no one was there. *Strange,* I thought. *I know I heard it.* A prickly sensation went up the back of my neck.

The peculiar phenomenon occurred several days in a row: the eerie whistle, then the unsettling feeling that someone was following me. One morning I was running late, so I decided to take a shortcut down a shady side street. I heard it again—that horrible whistle. This time, a sense of dread seized me.

When I slowly turned around, my eyes locked onto a robe-clad figure standing a few yards away. Around eight feet tall, he wore a long, white robe. His white, shoulder-length hair was brushed back from his forehead, revealing strange features set in tightly stretched skin and cold blue eyes.

I stood frozen in place, not convinced he was real. "I'm here to help you," he said in a monotone voice. "I've been watching you since you were a small child." That was enough for me. I took off running, anxiously repeating the prayer that had sustained me all my young life, "*Our Father, which art in heaven, hallowed by Thy name, Thy kingdom come, Thy will be done….*"

That night, as I tried to sleep, I sensed a presence. I opened my eyes and "he" was there, hovering. I shook myself. "You're not dreaming," the figure said, reading my mind. "I've come to help you. I'm a celestial spirit assigned to you." He continued, "I've come to aid you in your destiny and teach you about the coming New Age."

"I am part of a group of twelve beings who live in a higher spiritual plane. We are more advanced than earth people…The counsel of twelve is responsible for releasing…higher knowledge and always chooses individuals who have certain abilities…We've been watching you. We've taken notice of your special gifts." Then he divulged, "Remember when you were a child and you used to leave your body?

I was there. I was in that special place you went to. I've known you all your life, and now it is time for us to merge energies."

As quickly as he had come, he disappeared. "Dear God," I whispered, clutching the sheets, "This can't be happening to me." Without any Christian foundation to build on, I mistakenly lumped all supernatural phenomena under the vague term "God." But there were positive and negative forces to the supernatural universe. Surely God was the positive energy. The other stuff … well, I didn't really know what to do with it.

I went to the university library where I looked up books on psychic encounters. For hours on end I would sit cross-legged on the floor in the narrow aisles, a pile of dusty books around me. Through my research I learned, to my relief, that many people had experienced similar encounters. These celestial spirits were called spirit guides, and they were supposed to elevate a person into greater realms of spirituality.

Psychic things began to happen to me more often, even receiving a "glimpse" of the bloody body of a woman murdered in a house rented by one of my friends. He later informed me that it had happened just like I saw in my vision.

I went to a psychology professor hoping he could help me. Dr. Lands was familiar with parapsychology, so he listened to all my experiences, then began testing my level of psychic ability. He held up cards for me to tell what shape, number or color was on the other side. I succeeded at every test. As we talked, I felt the "stalker" enter the room. By now I could converse with it in my mind. He said, "You can't shut me out, Robin. You and I are meant to be one. You belong to me. The universe can be touched by you."

Noticing my fixation on something unseen, the doctor excitedly asked, "Is he here? Is he saying anything?" I responded, "He said I can't shut him out and that the universe can be touched by me."

Taken aback, Dr. Lands said, "Ask what he means by that." The spirit responded, "Tell the doctor that a quantum leap in the consciousness of man is coming to the whole earth, and that you have been chosen to assist us in our mission to bring the whole earth into one mind, one religion—the New Age." I hurried away from the room. I didn't care about the human race taking quantum leaps into the future—I just wanted out.

Meeting Marilyn

I knew something had to happen soon or I would lose my mind. I decided to hike up a mountain to "the slab" (a large piece of concrete way out in the woods, apparently poured for the foundation of a home never built). It was a perfect place to meditate, which I had begun to take seriously, practicing twice a day.

I sat down in my usual posture, the sunlight bathing me with its golden warmth. Everything was so peaceful: the sounds of nature all around me. I emptied my mind and opened myself to become one with the trees, the sky, the sun, the universe. I felt light and free. Then I heard it—a lilting voice—not human, but not belonging to my "tormentor" either.

"I will help you. Come up with me higher." The voice sounded soft, feminine. "Who are you?" I asked. "I am Marilyn. I've come to save you from the evil that's tried to destroy you." Attracted by the comforting voice I kept listening. "The evil came to hurt you. He's from the dark side. Stay with me, and he'll not harm you." Suddenly a brilliant, white light hovered over me. *This must be Marilyn,* I thought.

"God is us. We are God. There are good energies, and there are evil energies. What you open yourself up to is what you become." My mind seemed to be speaking on its own, whispering secret truth. Within a few months I was able to see a vague image of Marilyn in my mind whenever I meditated. I grew to trust the gentle voice that seemed infinitely wiser than me.

Dancing With Destiny

One day I passed the gym on my way to the journalism building and saw a dance class in progress. Something about the movement of the dancers made me stop and gaze. "You want to be a dancer, don't you?" said the voice, reading my thoughts. "You can." The scene mesmerized me—the mirrors, the beat of the music, the rows of sweaty dancers in leotards and leg-warmers. The instructor looked up from her warm-up routine and our eyes connected. She walked up and said the same words I'd just heard, then she added, "I can make you a professional dancer in four years if you're willing to give me 20 hours a week."

The next day, I was on the front row of that class. It quickly became my passion. At the end of the first quarter, part of my final exam was to choreograph a complete dance routine. It flowed perfectly. When I was finished, the other dancers even broke into spontaneous cheers. I glanced at Jackie, my teacher. Her face was beaming. She sent me a folded note,

A+++ Let's have lunch.

When we met, she invited me to join her dance company. Normally, no one got to dance professionally after just a few months of training. I almost laughed out loud with joy. "I'll take it!" Half an hour later, walking back to my dorm, Marilyn spoke to me, "See? I told you you could do it." I smiled and flew up the stairs—taking them two at a time.

Ticket to Hollywood

The thick fog obscured the highway as I drove toward Hollywood that spring morning of 1979. I was going to my first professional dance audition. Marilyn had promised I would become a star. As I rounded a curve, she spoke. "Today you will get this job and it will be your ticket to Los Angeles. Just go with the flow, and do as I tell you." "Yes, Marilyn," I said.

Five hours later I pulled in front of the Debbie Reynolds Studio in North Hollywood. Cars were crammed into every conceivable parking space around the large warehouse facility. The audition room was filled with 500 to 600 girls. I checked my appearance in the mirror, lifting my chin a little higher. What did I have to worry about? Didn't I already know what the outcome would be?

I felt the choreographer's eyes on me as I danced. When the music stopped, he nodded his head "yes," a sign that I was one of eight dancers he chose for a one-year contract to dance on the country-western television specials for the producer of "Solid Gold." I whispered, "Thank you, Marilyn."

Within a few weeks I moved to Hollywood and rented an apartment located right underneath the famous Hollywood sign. That night, Marilyn appeared to me in a dream. Until then I'd seen only hazy images of her in my mind's eye. In my dream I was looking out my apartment window, when I heard her voice behind me. Turning, I saw the slinky form of Marilyn Monroe lounging on my new sofa, a glass of champagne in her hand. "Don't look so surprised," the spirit said, laughing cattily. "Now let me tell you what to do to succeed in this town." Her first instruction was for me to dye my hair platinum blonde. I complied the next day.

From that time on, Marilyn was no longer just a voice. She appeared throughout my days in a physical apparition that only I could see. Years whizzed by. By the mid-1980s, my life was careening at a hectic pace. Then one evening, I received a phone call at a friend's apartment. I was puzzled. I hadn't given anyone the number.

"Hello, is this Robin Harry?" a man's voice asked. "Yes." The caller identified himself as Steven Baker, a prominent film director. "This is going to sound strange, but I need to find out who you are," he said, chuckling apologetically. "When I came back from lunch today, your name and number were on my private list of people to call. I have no earthly idea how they got there." By the end of the conversation, I had an appointment the next day.

As I drove through the manicured streets of Beverly Hills, Marilyn detailed what would happen. She informed me this was only a stepping stone to get me in with somebody much bigger. She was right. By the time we'd finished dinner together, he was planning on introducing me to Marvin Schlesser, a famous agent in a leading talent agency. I was there the next day by 9:45 a.m. After a lengthy meeting, Marvin told he would represent me professionally. I glanced over his head. There Marilyn was, smiling, her red lips parting slightly. Everything grew quiet.

Marvin glanced around the room and softly spoke, "Do you have a spirit guide?" "Yes," I said, waiting for his reaction. "Is it Marilyn Monroe?" His discernment startled me. "Yes," I half-whispered. "Is she here now?" I nodded. "I used to do some work for her when she was alive." My heart was thumping wildly as I stepped on an elevator an hour later. I thought how lucky I was to have Marilyn on my side. Clearly, the last two days had been arranged by her.

By that time I was convinced that my imminent stardom would become a platform for me to share my enlightenment with the world. The quantum leap, the one-world religion, spirituality: these were all themes of my vision for the future. During hours of meditation, Marilyn had shared those concepts with me.

A few days later, my tarot card reader, Sam, invited me to a private meeting of psychics in Mill Valley, a New Age Mecca located in northern California. I'd been attending these types of meetings regularly, learning all I could about the New Age. This meeting was hosted by Mrs. Langley, a powerful woman in the movement. Her guest was a well-known medium, with an ordinary housewife appearance. I was one of about 20 or so guests.

"Now, she is going to channel the *descended* master," the assistant said. As the medium in front of us opened her mouth and spoke, a wave of nausea washed over me. The voice was deep and masculine. In a commanding monotone, it told us how to become more one with the universe—more one with "God." I'd witnessed numerous channelings, but this one frightened me.

When the session ended, the medium looked directly at me and walked out. After the guests went into the refreshment area, the medium's assistant tapped my shoulder. "The spirit wants to speak to you," she said, her face expressionless. I followed her down a stone path to a small, star-shaped building. As I entered the "star room," that I later learned was in the shape of a pentagram (a symbol used in Wicca, neo-paganism and satanism), the sickening sensation gripped me again.

The spirit spoke out of the medium, "You will lead people. You will become famous. You have already connected with the man. He will help you…" The voice continued, describing in remarkable detail my past, present, and future.

Shortly after, for some reason, my relationship with Marilyn began to sour. I began to catch glimmers of a hostile side to her nature. At times, she grew argumentative, snapping at me if I didn't jump to do her bidding. Then she did something outrageous. She forced an entry into my body, while I was kissing my boyfriend, Brian, as if she wanted to kiss him *through* me. He pulled back aghast, realizing what had happened. Rubbing his eyes, he said, "O my God, this is too weird. I wasn't kissing you Robin. It wasn't your face. I saw Marilyn Monroe." I was furious. Marilyn had invaded me without permission. I shouted angry insults and threats to her. She vanished for the night.

Over the next few months I continued attending meetings with Mrs. Langley's crowd, though I began sensing an emerging evil in their midst. Simultaneously, it was becoming uncomfortably clear that Marilyn and I were in a power struggle for my mind—and my soul. I was determined not to let her win.

The Accident

The time was 6 p.m. I'd already put in a ten-hour day on the set of a Coca-Cola commercial; next I had to rush to Beverly Hills, where I was working part-time as a waitress in a hip Italian restaurant. I hurried in the back entrance. Three feet above the ground was a large utility closet with a heavy, six-inch-thick, solid-oak door where I stashed my purse. As always, I pulled it open carefully because the hinges were loose. "Hey, baby!" It was Tony, the sleazy manager who tried to dress like Fonzy. "You're late," he snapped. "I was working on a commercial, OK? I'm sorry," I said apologetically.

"Look who just walked in," a fellow waitress said, looking starry-eyed. "They're in your section." It was a very influential director and the other was the star of a popular nighttime television series. Everybody turned and looked. *Someday everyone will do that for me,* I thought as I walked up to the table. The celebrity watched me as I approached. He nudged the director next to him, whispering something to Tony. They all chuckled. All three men took a long, sweeping look at me. I felt violated, as if I were standing there naked. Blood rushed to my face. I hoped it would go unnoticed.

I went to the bathroom and took a couple of hits of cocaine. "Thank God for drugs," I said aloud. Asking someone else to fill the drink order for me, I retreated to the kitchen. An inner voice said, "You can't let them get to you like that! Get out and take that order!" It was a command accompanied by an invisible push. The hostess looked startled as I grabbed the tray from her hand.

She backed away a few steps. Then someone shouted, "Look out!" A split second later, the nine-foot-high, 150-pound utility closet door fell out of the wall and came crashing down on me. I screamed as it struck my skull, then I crumpled to the ground. Someone spoke firmly, "Get her out of here before anyone notices!" The last thing I remember is being carried out to the back seat of a car.

Sterile Walls, Shattered Dreams

I came to in the hospital, gazing at several IVs hooked to my arm. "God, where am I?" I said shakily, "I can't feel my body." I was shaking with a seizure. The nurse rushed in with a hypodermic needle. She administered the drug and the shaking ceased. Dr. Sellerman told me I had suffered major damage to the motor control center in my brain. Day after day, I fought the wrenching pain and violent shaking that seized my body, each seizure remedied by a shot of Demerol. One of the worst thoughts plaguing my mind was the realization that I was "set up" for the accident, that the "voice" had purposefully led me right into the path of danger. Maybe it wasn't Marilyn's voice, but there was definitely a supernatural cause.

After a month they moved me to the Shuman Rehabilitation Clinic. "You don't know how fortunate you are to be going here," said Dr. Sellerman as he walked by my wheelchair. I could barely lift my head to smile feebly and say, "Let's go."

Rehab started at 9 a.m. each morning—speech therapy, physical therapy, occupational therapy, and biofeedback therapy. I would finish by four o'clock in the afternoon. With the physical exertion of therapy, I was consuming even more pain mediation than before and quickly became addicted. Even though nearly two months had passed since the accident, I was still having four to five seizures a day. My whole body would shake violently for half an hour.

Therapy was grueling, but it worked. The day to attempt walking finally came. With a therapist on each side and one in front, they stood me up. When I took my first few steps the room full of therapists, hospital workers and friends exploded with cheers and wild clapping. "I did it," I said to Dr. Sellerman, "I really did it," tears streaming down my face. I was on cloud nine. I was still a long way away from normal, but it was a start. Not long after that, I returned home.

When my friend Jeri pulled us into the driveway, I looked up and saw the Hollywood sign on the hill. "What a joke," I hissed. "It should say Hellwood, home of broken dreams and discarded dreamers." Life was overwhelming. Confinement to the wheelchair, the excruciating pain and the constant seizures—it all took its toll on me mentally and emotionally.

Encountering the True God

One day I just couldn't take it anymore. I pulled myself out of bed and made my way to the kitchen, bracing on the furniture. I opened the cabinet and saw the bottles of pain pills. The thought hit me. "That's it. I'll take an overdose of pills." Just in time, the loud ringing of the telephone interrupted my thoughts. The answering machine clicked on. "Hey, Robin, are you there?" a familiar voice said. "Do you want to go to church tonight? I thought maybe you could use some company. If you do, give me a call."

It was Prescott, the bass player in my boyfriend's rock band. Ever since he'd become "born again," he hadn't been the same. I looked at the bottles of pills again. *Maybe I'll just go to church with Prescott and then do it when I get back.*

It took three hours for me to get ready, then Prescott called. His car had broken down on the freeway and he couldn't pick me up. "Maybe it isn't such a good idea for me to come anyway," I said. "No, Robin, you've just got to come!" he responded with urgency in his voice.

Leaving the wheelchair just inside the front door, I slowly made my way down the three steps in front of my house and over to the driveway. Hollywood Presbyterian happened to be just three blocks down the hill from my apartment. Somehow I coasted the car safely all the way down. As I pulled in the parking lot, I noticed a young man with jet-black hair who was dressed in a suit standing in front of the small chapel. His name was Christian Harfouche. I didn't know I was looking at the man who one day would be my husband.

I struggled out of my car and immediately felt the presence of an unseen power all around. I had always been sensitive to spiritual feelings, but this was different. I knew something extraordinary was about to happen. As the people sang, they lifted their hands to God. I was touched by the beauty of their voices blending together. Fresh tears poured down my cheeks. Then a realization hit me. "I'm not in pain," I confided to Prescott, my eyes wide with disbelief.

When the singing was over, a man walked to the front and began to speak. As he preached, his words pricked my heart. He told the simple story of how Jesus came and died on the cross of Calvary, how He gave His life for me so that I could spend eternity in Heaven. Something leaped inside me. I knew that for the first time in my life I was hearing the truth.

Suddenly, Marilyn's image intruded into my mind. I watched in horror as a deceiving façade peeled away. Gone was the svelte feminine form, the platinum hair, the pretty face. In their place was a hideous black creature with sunken features and twisted, clawlike hands. Its bulging yellow eyes glowed with evil. No one had to tell me. I knew intuitively: "Marilyn" was an evil spirit that had lied to me and wanted to use me to deceive others.

I opened my eyes to avoid the horrible image. At the same instant I heard a scream inside my head. "You wouldn't go all the way! You could have had it all. I'm the one who wanted you dead. You knew too much! You knew all about the plan!" I heard one last scream, then silence. The spirit's grip on me was gone.

The preacher stopped speaking and asked those who wanted to accept Jesus to come forward. "I need God," I whispered, as I pulled myself toward the aisle, "the real God."

"You are being healed," I heard the minister say as I fell backward, hit by some invisible power. Sobs racked my body. I couldn't control myself. When I got up I was astonished. All of the muscles in my body worked. They were supple, not clenched into rock-hard knots. For the first time in months I could turn my neck from side to side. My legs felt limber and strong again. I could walk normally.

When I returned to my apartment, I was not prepared for what hit me. "*This is God,*" I heard in my spirit like an audible voice, "*You have been healed.*" This voice was different than the others that used to torment me. Then God gave me specific instructions. He told me to throw out all the occult paraphernalia I had accumulated over the years: my crystals, books, tarot cards, New Age tapes, everything. All that remained on my bookshelf was a little paperback Bible. Then God let me know, "*You will go through two days of drug withdrawals. On Monday you will be well. Do not worry, because I will be with you all the time.*"

The next 48 hours were the most difficult of my life. But after it was over, I was free. Then I attended a home prayer meeting. The man who was preaching the night I was healed was there. He said, "I knew you would come tonight… When I was praying earlier this evening, the Lord showed me He was going to fill you with the Holy Spirit…" Before he even got the word "Spirit" out, I was knocked flat on the floor by the same power I'd felt the night I was healed. Suddenly, I heard the sound of my own voice, but the words coming from my mouth were not in English. I was speaking in tongues, just as they did in the early church.

Days later, I drove to the studio in West Hollywood where I had taught so many dance classes over the past several years. I reserved the second story dance room for a couple of hours just for me. The memories flooded my mind. I had no music, just the music in my soul. Holding my breath, I started to move in soft, balletic steps. I pirouetted once, then twice, then a third time. Joy bubbled up inside me, and I was all over the room, dancing and leaping and twirling and kicking as high as my head. I laughed in sheer delight as I moved about the room. I danced as I had never danced before.

It was an expression of thanks, of utter praise, to God and God alone. I was so glad to finally know my Heavenly Father. I heard Him speak to me in His still voice, "I am the director of your life now… and I will write the script."

Commentary by Mike Shreve

The primary theme addressed by the spirits Robin Harfouche encountered was idea of a "*coming New Age,*" but what does that mean?

This concept is based on astrology: the study of the supernatural influence stars and planets are said to have over human affairs. In astrological teaching, the sun passes through 12 houses as it travels around the earth. Each "house" represents an age lasting around 2,200 years. (Incidentally, this belief became popular when it was commonly held that the sun actually *did* revolve around the earth.)

According to many astrologers and New Agers, the human race is presently moving from the Piscean Age (an age of intellectual advance and the rise of religion) into the Aquarian Age (an age of enlightenment, spirituality and peace on the planet). Though some say the Age of Aquarius has already begun, many who adhere to this mindset feel we are still in a transitional stage—to be marked by great social upheaval, cataclysmic happenings, and a worldwide spiritual awakening.

When I was a New Ager (though we didn't use the term back then) I actually connected the coming of a "New Age" with the "coming of Christ." However, I interpreted that event quite differently than I do now. Like many of my mentors and peers, I spiritualized it—promoting the idea that the "second coming of Christ" was not the return of an individual, but rather, an awakening of Christ consciousness within the masses.

I explained to my students that the transition into the Age of Aquarius would be a gradual shift in planetary consciousness—as thousands, then millions, then billions realize their own divinity (the understanding that "we are God') and their oneness with the universe and each other. Then, in a sense, the "scales will tilt" and the whole world will shift over into an age of universal awareness and enlightenment, a time when love and harmony will prevail everywhere, a time when wars will cease, a time when all nations and religions will be one, a time when many of the world's crises will be solved. It should be mentioned that there are many alternate ideas among New Agers concerning this crucial era. Some believe in an actual individual , a "messianic avatar" (an enlightened "world teacher") who will emerge on the global stage to bring healing and unity: politically, economically, religiously and spiritually. Some even identify him as "Maitreya."

Though there are some similarities, the biblical view is much different than the various New Age forecasts for the future. First of all, Christianity does not subscribe to the idea that human beings *are* God. So the pivotal turning point will not be some gradual global awakening of consciousness as people discover their own personal divinity. Neither will it be an avataric individual, presently alive in this world, who will eventually achieve spiritual and/or political recognition and global dominance. Instead, it will hinge on a powerful and momentary event—the literal, bodily return of Jesus Christ, *"the image of the invisible God"*—who will personally and visibly appear *"in flaming fire,"* with all *"His mighty angels"* and with *"ten thousands of His saints"*

(Col. 1:15, 2 Thess. 1:7-8, Jude 1:14). *"Every eye will see Him"* when He comes to establish His Lordship in this world (Rev. 1:7). Metaphorically, Isaiah foretold that in that day, *"the light of the sun will be like the light of seven days"* and Zechariah foretold that the Messiah will descend upon the Mount of Olives in Jerusalem and the mountain will split in two (see Isa. 30:26, Zech. 14:4).

Jesus (Yeshua) will then triumphantly pass through the eastern gate of the wall of Jerusalem and assume His reign on temple mount, to establish the Kingdom of God on earth for a thousand years (the Millennial Kingdom). The dead in Christ will be resurrected and given glorified bodies. Living believers will be changed into eternal forms *"in a moment, in the twinkling of an eye"* (1 Cor. 15:52). These benefits of the coming of the Messiah will not be poured out universally on everyone regardless of their character, religion or faith, but only on *"those who eagerly wait for Him"* and confess Jesus as Lord of their lives (Heb. 9:28).

In this coming era of heaven on earth, wars will cease, sickness and poverty will be no more, and such love will permeate the world that even nature will be healed: lambs and lions will coexist peacefully (see Isa. 11:6). Such an all-encompassing global transformation will not be effected by any other "messianic figure" predicted in another religion, but only by the compassionate Savior who paid the supreme price of dying on the cross for the sins of the human race, the glorious Overcomer who conquered death and the grave. He alone has the right, the privilege and the authority to restore this world to a paradise once again. He has promised that those who love and serve Him will actually reign with Him, as fully manifested sons of God, during the Kingdom Age, then into the next era, called the New Creation (the New Heaven and the New Earth). That final magnificent phase will be eternal and unchanging (see Rev. 21:1).

Let me reemphasize, I did say *"eternal and unchanging."* Astrological ages are altogether opposite. They are only temporary phases, fluctuating in a predictable way. They are cyclical, only lasting around 2,200 years. No final solution is ever reached. All Far Eastern religions embrace this cyclical view of the future, though the details vary greatly. These "ages" are repeated over and over again, *ad infinitum*, resulting in global conditions that ascend and/or descend, ranging from terrible to wonderful, then back to terrible again. Times of global peace and enlightenment never last.

Quite the contrary, the biblical forecast is for a FINAL CHANGE that will result in absolute perfection and infinite excellence—an everlasting inheritance granted to those who are in covenant with the true God.

So there you have it: the two main scenarios from which to choose—a temporary New Age or a permanent New Creation. If it was up to you to make the decision, which one of these would you choose as your future destiny?

As they say, that's a no-brainer.

About the Writer

Robin Harfouche and her husband, Christian Harfouche, pastor the on-fire Miracle Faith Center in Pensacola, Florida. They have a global outreach, ministering around the world in mass gatherings, and also by means of television with their power-packed telecast, *Miracles Today*. Most of the information contained in this chapter was obtained from the book on Robin's story, also titled *From Hollywood to Heaven*.

Email: info@globalrevival.com

Website: www.globalrevival.com

Chapter 2

A Modern Spiritual Odyssey

By Stanley Petrowski

*A student of the world's mystery religions
encounters God in the Himalayan Mountains!*

I won't belabor the vagaries of my childhood. Suffice it to say that they were filled with violence, fear, and confusion. Inner-city Philadelphia was quite adept at nurturing such a climate. I escaped in 1964 by enlisting in the U.S. Army at the age of 17. Seeing more of the world was enticing to me.

Eighteen months of my tour was on a missile site on the island of Okinawa. While there, I busied myself with a correspondence school, majoring in psychology. My mind was a fertile field. At that point, the study of human nature seemed to be a key to understanding. After reading *Walden Two* by B.F. Skinner, I became excited at the prospect of creating a pure environment to produce the perfect man to usher in a golden age of human history. It was an unfounded euphoria, but it paved the way for further quests.

Seeking more adventure, I volunteered for the war zone. My time was spent pulling guard duty in an ammunition dump and keeping the night patrols. I saw plenty of napalm, night flares, and marijuana. All my waking hours were spent in a drug-altered state. One day, a Red Cross helicopter showed up at camp to inform me of an emergency leave. My mother had died. Unfortunately, that period of time is a blur to me. The dazed stupor I was in dulled my senses. After the funeral, I decided to return to Vietnam a married man. So I wedded my teenage girlfriend and headed back to the war.

In August of 1967, I left my "arduous" military career behind and entered civilian life. There was a gnawing emptiness that haunted me. It didn't matter if it was school or my pursuit of creative arts; every aspect of life seemed stained by a glaring lack of something true and real. Of course, the chant of the sixties was the supposed answer, "Turn on, tune in, and drop out." Being awash in the head-trips of the time, my interests switched from psychology to spirituality. Names like Buddha, Lao Tsu, and a host of others became part of my vocabulary.

I came across one publication that illustrated eternity in a profound way. On the plain white page of a Zen Buddhism book was a circle. The caption read, "The circle is the symbol of eternity. It has no beginning or end." Somehow that became proof to me of an infinite spiritual realm. "Forever" became tangible to me with a simple piece of artwork. I was compelled to take radical steps that would alter my future forever. I felt there must be answers to life. I quit school, left my job, and started hitchhiking.

My Introduction to Hallucinogenics

I made it to the coastal town of Wildwood, New Jersey. Before dawn, I walked down the empty boardwalk. Only one shop was open. Looking in, I was surprised to see a familiar face from a "beatnik" hangout in downtown Philadelphia. Steve was a low-key person with a gentle, friendly way. We talked philosophy and religion. The idealism of the times was evident in our conversation.

"I want to share half of what I have in my possession with you. If everyone did this, all would have enough," I proposed. I took my last bit of money, bought him a sandwich and coffee and felt good about myself. He said, "I have something to share with you. Have you ever been on a trip? I've got a double hit of STP." With that he opened a small piece of aluminum foil that held a white tablet. Cutting it in half, he said, "Put this under your tongue."

As the sun came up, the powerful hallucinogen started taking effect. The spiritual dimension I was ardently seeking seemed to unfold before my eyes. I became sensitized to higher levels of energy as though I had passed through a door of some other world. It was incapacitating. Someone put a Beatles album on and things really began to deepen. My senses began blurring and cross-circuiting into a mixture of sound and color. Eighteen hours rushed past. My consciousness slipped out of the realm of reality. Only the outline of my body could be seen. There were no objects at all, no up or down. I was transparent, the ethereal outline of my body burning with blue flames.

Leaving the blue fire, I had the strange experience of watching myself pass through the colors of the rainbow. Each color level had its own unique symbols and level of consciousness. Soon, I burst into a realm of blinding light. Brighter and brighter, faster and faster went the pace. Then there appeared an intensely luminous, golden Buddha seated in the lotus position. I surged past it into a realm of cosmic bliss and a state of *thoughtless awareness*.

Then in a flash I dropped down from an altered state of consciousness into a normal frame of mind. What happened to me? It was morning. The drugged state captured an entire day of my life. It came and went, but its influence remained, compelling me to pursue spiritual understanding.

Becoming a "Flower Child"

Had I stumbled across the answer to my utopian dreams? Was it really as simple as dropping a hit of acid or some other mind-bending drug? Apparently an entire generation of people believed that. I met a few of Steve's friends heading out to Haight-Ashbury in the San Francisco Bay area. "Come along. We've got room in the car."

In a matter of hours I was swept along with an entire generation to become a "flower child." No more evil. No more violence or war, just peace, love, and joy. Commune after commune we visited along the way accommodated this New Age euphoria. Drugs flowed like candy. Food we had in abundance. Relationships came and went according to the drift of the moment. But it was the mysteries of spiritual and psychic activity that engulfed my attention.

Being impelled to enter the realms of light once again, I took many drugs in a short period of time. These chemicals soon made a shambles of my mental faculties. At one point, I went to the filming of a movie at a local music hall and arrived to see a fantastic light show. Someone handed me five double hits of STP. Then another person gave me some Hawaiian wood rose seeds. I ate them all. In a matter of minutes I knew it was not going to go well and I was going to lose consciousness.

Amid the din of rock "n" roll and flashing lights, waves of anxiety swept over me. Like a raving maniac I ran out of the auditorium into San Francisco's Golden Gate Park. I managed to crawl behind some dense shrubbery and collapse. I laid on my back, hands curled on my chest, and lost all sense of the outside world. Unlike my first experience, this one cast me powerless into an abyss. No sound, no light, only endless, fathomless darkness. I had entered death and was unable to leave.

Many hours later, my consciousness returned. Wearing only blue jeans, I made it out of the park. Terribly disabled, I found a group of people sitting on the steps to their house. "Come on in man. You're just having a bad trip." They sat me down between two large speakers and handed me a joint. Soon loud raucous music was blasting. Terror gripped me. I fled. Babbling like a mindless idiot, I sat in a heap on a downtown San Francisco sidewalk, weeping and unable to communicate.

Night was upon the city. I roamed trying to find a safe haven. I came across some old condemned houses. Upon entering, I found a strange person already residing there. He said I could stay in one of the rooms. They were all filled with debris. The walls were covered with the sayings of Bob Dylan and other revered prophets, philosophers, and sages of the day.

Unable to sleep, I looked out the window to see what I thought was a warning of impending doom. The buildings appeared to be heaving under the undulations of a massive earthquake. I was again driven to run and managed to get a ride to Berkeley across the Bay. Along the way, I picked up a copy of an underground newspaper, *The San Francisco Oracle*. On the back page was a copy of Psalm 23 super-imposed on an image of Jesus crowned with thorns. I began to frantically repeat the psalm over and over.

By a quirk of fate, I found myself in the middle of the most intense night of the famous Berkeley riots. Black Panthers, the SDS, the SLA and the general populace were looting and destroying everything in sight. The crack of firearms shocked me all the more. Driven again by panic, I escaped, hitchhiking out of town.

The Glow of a Spiritual Light

In three days I found myself in Portland, Oregon, and managed to locate a Christian crash pad. Bedraggled, I entered. The serenity of the occupants impressed me. A remarkable, spiritual glow radiated from the attendants' faces. I stayed, eventually acquiring a job and vaguely grasping that the biblical message my new-found friends shared was their source of joy.

So I went down to the Columbia River to be immersed (baptized). I committed my life to Jesus and began to gain ground. However, as my life began to stabilize, my concerns shifted to the shattered pieces I'd left behind in Philadelphia. No one knew of my whereabouts. Surely it was right to return and make amends. My whirlwind tour of the counter-culture had taken a year or so. It was clear upon my return that I wasn't alone in having my world turned upside down. Old friends had also been swept up in the frenzied drug feed. I hardly recognized many of them. While I was gone, my father had died. My wife had thrown off any regard for our marriage (understandably) and was pregnant by a friend. The pieces I'd hoped to reassemble didn't even exist anymore.

So I purposed to start anew. My travels had exposed me to the idea I could improve the quality of my life, reversing the effects of drugs and a lifetime of junk food, through natural foods. I spent quite a bit of time studying naturopathic therapies and herbal remedies, and met a few fellows who were interested in starting a health food store. We did, and soon had a large constituency enjoying our homemade soups, breads, carrot juice and whole grains. Our store attracted a wide range of people embracing a variety of spiritual perspectives. I took great care to closely inspect all of these philosophical and religious views.

One book that caught my attention was *The Aquarian Gospel of Jesus Christ*. It revealed the so-called "hidden" years of the Messiah. It described Him visiting the Far East, Egypt, and many of the world's mystery schools, finally attaining great mystical stature, then returning to the Holy Land for public ministry.

This idea became a catalyst, launching me into many spiritual disciplines—from eating (Zen macrobiotics), to astrology, tarot cards, and an intense regime of meditation. Every related publication became food to my hungry mind: *The Upanishads*, Khalil Gibran, *Tao Te Ching*, a large cosmological volume called *Urantia,* and both *The Egyptian* and *Tibetan Books of the Dead.* Hatha yoga and mantra yoga filled my days. In one meditation session I hovered over my body and was able to observe all the objects in the room. "Surely," I thought, "I am learning the things Jesus learned, on the Great Path of Enlightenment."

The urge to find a solution for personal and collective healing overwhelmed me. Daily I poured over the "sacred" writings of the various epochs and cultures of the world. My soul grasped for greater insight and doorways of spiritual initiation. Was I part of something bigger? Was the utopian Aquarian Age appearing?

Into the Mountains

March of 1969 I once again abandoned the mundane activities of daily life. The health food business was prospering, but the unsettled state of my heart beckoned me to continue my spiritual quest. I landed in the Rocky Mountains of Colorado. Purposing to live as a religious recluse, I wore a woolen-hooded robe, hand-stitched out of army blankets. My diet consisted of brown rice and any foods I foraged in the wilds. I built a little lean-to for protection from the ravages of the high country's early spring weather.

Quickly my life settled into a predictable routine. Each morning, I immersed myself in the icy spring that flowed nearby. After thawing out, I'd breakfast, pray, and study. Not a day would go by without casting the *I Ching* (a form of Chinese divination: casting yarrow stalks and interpreting them by the Chinese *Book of Changes*). The only adversity I encountered was a squirrel's persistent ransacking of my grain stash.

One morning in late April, I was awakened by a vivid dream in which I was told to leave my mountain sanctuary. So I hid my supplies and began descending the mountain. I had not seen anyone my entire stay. Even the old dirt roads were overgrown. Not very far from my camp I encountered a young man in a vehicle, staring off into the grand mountain view. It startled both of us. He smiled, saying, "I guess I was supposed to meet you here!" After I told him my dream, he agreed to take me to Colorado Springs.

Meeting the Ascended Masters

Soon I became friends with a number of "searchers" in the area. Though we'd all taken drugs, we left that option behind in our pursuit of truth. Several of us decided to visit the headquarters of the Summit Lighthouse, later to be called the Church Universal and Triumphant. They incorporated ideas and religious practices from all major religions and schools of mysticism. This group was to play a big role in the next phase of my life.

My first visit was highlighted with an intense awareness of the spiritual elements that surrounded this organization. They claimed to be in contact with a spiritual hierarchy of great men and women. These "Ascended Masters" supposedly had attained enlightenment and were transmitting knowledge and assistance to the human race for its freedom in preparation for a New Age. Among this august host of gods, goddesses, masters, angelic beings and inter-dimensional intelligences were Jesus, Buddha, Lao Tsu, and just about every deity and enlightened being presented by every religion, myth, and mystery school of the world.

Mark and Elizabeth Prophet, the Messengers of the "Masters," formed the organization and were riding the crest of the wave of interest in alternative religions of the late sixties and early seventies. The headquarters consisted of a turn-of-the-century mansion (the Monastery), located in the high-end district of Broadmore called La Tourelle. Soon I was on staff and began participating in an intense regimen, meditating and chanting up to 16 hours a day.

Day and night I also assisted Elizabeth as she edited copious amounts of literature. Because of the status of Mark and Elizabeth as Messengers of the Great White Brotherhood, it seemed proper to them to have guardians. So, along with several others, I attended the Messengers wherever they went, always on guard. Frequently, we slept on the floor outside their luxuriant master bedroom.

The spiritual beings that were the real backbone of this religious group regularly expressed themselves through the Messengers. Weekly oracles and quarterly conferences, filled with outpourings of teachings, were the heartbeat of the organization. Regularly, gurus, spiritual teachers, pundits, and politicians attended and added to the meetings. It seemed as though the organization was a point of confluence for the energies that were molding the present social and political climate.

The essence of the teachings revolved around the notion that each being has at the core of his or her consciousness a "divine spark" that is intrinsically a part of "God." Because reincarnation and the doctrine of karma were also held, the awareness of this divine nature was said to be clouded by deeds, dark forces, and illusion that must be escaped. Mantras and prayers, thought forms and visualizations, meditations and spiritual exercises, faithfully applied, were said to grant spiritual liberation. I personally experienced many of the promised outcomes, including the awakening of the "*shakti*" force of the "*kundalini.*"

Several world tours were taken to key places of spiritual or political importance. I recall on the Autumn Equinox of 1972 scaling the sides of the Great Pyramid of Giza with three of my comrades to perform rituals at its peak. The full moon was in Aries, the sun in Libra, and all of the planets were in "auspicious" places. Our intent was to work in conjunction with the Masters to raise the world out of the mire of ignorance into a New Age of global change. Ironically, during my time there, one of my rituals consisted of breaking bread and drinking a sip of wine and asking Master Jesus to cause these elements to become to me what they should be. It is difficult to express how all of these things completely engulfed my soul.

Unraveling of Spiritual Discipline

In late 1972, Mark Prophet died of a stroke and the entire operation fell into the hands of Elizabeth. The shakeup was profound. An oppressive stress permeated my days. I also found myself immersed in impure and divergent thoughts. It was customary for me to afflict myself. I wore a horse hair shirt, a belt of woven thorns, and regularly flagellated myself in an attempt to subdue my carnal nature. For some reason, at Mark's death these primal carnal urges intensified. My youthful vigor at the age of 25 was breaking loose, violating my years of careful control.

A young lady on staff told me she was "practicing" on me to capture my heart. Though I never consummated the relationship, I may as well have. The affair broke me so utterly down that it felt like my psyche was imploding. My vows of celibacy were now being resisted by raging passion. I walked around numb for weeks, only to finally acknowledge my inability to maintain the level of God consciousness I presumed I had attained. So I left the Summit Lighthouse and went back to the wild regions of the Colorado Rocky Mountains. Though I had terribly failed the cause, eventually I felt a kind of reconciliation with the beings who were "setting the world free." It was their will; they wanted me out of there! But what next?

The MacKays

Soon after, I met the MacKay family and developed a deep relationship with them. They were very much like most of the upper middle class of that era. Mr. MacKay was a successful businessman in the energy industry. Mrs. MacKay was an amiable lady with a keen interest in spiritual things. Suddenly a barefooted, white-robed mystic showed up in their lives. I stayed at their house in a room they graciously provided. Being a renunciate, my only possessions were the clothes on my back. I had frequent conversations with them on philosophy and the mystery religions.

Mrs. MacKay, seeing my meager holdings and sincerity, was compelled one day to give me a thousand dollars. She said God had instructed her to do so. Persuaded that material possessions were a hindrance to my path, I refused. She insisted that the cashier's check would remain intact for my use at any time. I was in a quandary as to why God had moved her to act in this fashion.

Not long after this incident, during a late-night discussion of the many traditions that have filled human history, the room where we sat filled with a brilliant blue light. A large, luminous sphere appeared out of which a voice spoke. We sat entranced as a command was given to me, "Come and find me." Immediately I had a vision of the Himalayan Mountains.

Now the cashier's check made sense. The government of India was shutting its doors to many visitors. In the late 1960s, there had been a tremendous influx of seekers who, upon reaching India, were unable to care for themselves. So every effort was made to thoroughly screen individuals entering the country. I remember showing up at the travel agency dressed in traditional yogic garb. Against all odds, I had my papers in order within two weeks.

The Everest Trek

It was late summer when I arrived, stricken with a severe fever. Undaunted, I made my way to Vrindavan, identified as the birthplace of Krishna, one of India's best-known gods. I circumambulated the village three times and stayed at a Krishna ashram until my fever subsided. Afterward, I headed for Rishikesh, a Mecca for yogis, mendicants, and devotees of the myriads of Hindu, Buddhist, and other religious sects at the headwaters of the Ganges River. Next I traveled to Katmandu, located in a beautiful valley at the Himalayan foothills of Nepal.

There I began what is called "the Everest Trek." Between Katmandu and a small town named Bhadgoan in the same valley was a paved road about three miles long. It was the only one in the country at the time, and a private bus serviced it. The Nepalese people were mostly short in stature. When I entered the packed bus, I stood head and shoulders above the natives. Most of the men wore little black tight-fitting hats and black vests, a kind of cultural uniform. In the back of the bus stood a man in the traditional clothing, but uniquely different—he had blue eyes and stood taller than the rest.

He introduced himself with a strong, Australian accent, asking why I was in Nepal. No doubt he had seen many Europeans and Westerners on spiritual pilgrimages to these mountains. I told him how I was led to that land to search out my next spiritual teacher. He assured me he knew who I was looking for. Curious, I asked who that might be. His simple reply was, "Jesus Christ." I assumed his understanding of Jesus to be very different from mine, so our conversation was pleasant, but short-lived.

I exited the bus to begin a two-month walk through the lonely winding roads of this remote Himalayan region. The terrain was unforgiving, with steep climbs and treacherous jungle regions, broken up by intermittent domesticated areas with villages in their center. The ascents were often very abrupt, requiring a traversing type of climb rather than a direct route. My bare feet at this time were hardened enough to endure the hiking.

In spite of the majestic scenery, my attention was only slightly diverted. Maintaining a deep meditative mindset was my focus. When I would emerge from this trance-like state, at times, I would hardly know where I was or how far I'd gone. Nights passed as

I listlessly waited out a rainstorm, curled up in a little ball on the ground, engulfed in darkness and hoping for dawn.

Upon reaching a very large village area called Those Bazaar, I again became deathly ill, delirious with a fever. A gracious person took my offer to pay for refuge as I sought to recover. During that time I dreamed I was in a large, full theater. I sat in the front row, looking up at extremely tall, dark, red, velvet curtains. Next to me sat a young lady friend who was also waiting for the stage to open. Suddenly I was constrained to leave and pleaded with her to go with me. She obstinately refused, so I arose and began walking up the long walkway, grieving that I had no friend. To compound this, the people of the theater began raucously laughing at me because of my departure. As I was leaving, a light shown from above and a voice spoke, "I will be your friend." I was so deeply affected that I awoke to find the fever completely gone. Up and away I went, thanking my host who marveled at my recovery.

Soon I also contracted a violent stomach ailment. Quite ill, I arrived at the Tutenchilling Tibetan Buddhist Monastery. The grounds were abuzz with monks participating in various rituals. Before long, I found myself in their temple engaged in their chanting and drinking liquid from the silver-lined skull of a long-dead, supposed highly esteemed incarnation of Buddha.

How fantastically the place was enshrouded in every form of art depicting the varied aspects of this particular branch of Buddhism! Tanka paintings were everywhere. Prayer flags draped from the tops of every building. Worshipers constantly circled the grounds, zealously chanting mantras on their prayer beads. Mandalas and images of gods and Buddhas, exquisitely painted, adorned their walls.

Feeling the need to travel on, I set out for the Thangboche Monastery where I was told I would meet my teacher. By now my trek was well into the higher reaches of the Himalayas, above the timberline, in view of the majestic, always-white peaks of the border between Nepal and Tibet. The nights were cold and the rumble of avalanches could be heard in the distance.

As I drew near Thangboche, the view became intensely beautiful. Thousands of feet below were the green verdant jungles, pierced by the raging torrents of a river that showed pure white from my vantage point. Misty clouds would erupt from the jungle regions below and billow up the steep canyons, forming clouds of rainbow colors during sunset. The beauty was overwhelming.

I Must Have the Truth

It was in such an area that I stopped to meditate. I withdrew myself from all but that inner spiritual reality. In anguish of heart I began to cry out to God, to Buddha, to Jesus, to whoever would hear me! With much weeping and desperate brokenness of heart I wailed. Tears and soul-cry poured out of me. I must have the truth! Truly it was a cry from the utmost depths of my inner man, expressing in anguished sobs what words could not. I poured out my soul like water—as though I was mourning over the death of a loved one.

Like ice in a spring thaw, my ignorance began to melt. Knowledge to turn from darkness to light was bestowed on me. A spiritual door opened before me. As I entered, the LIGHT of LIFE flooded my inner being. A hideous weight and great shadow lifted from me. Peace washed over my soul. High above me stood a figure. As the sun appears through the clouds on an overcast day—so this brilliant form appeared to me. I had no doubt. This was JESUS (Yeshua), the Messiah.

Immediately, I knew that the experience of the blue light I had been following was a deception, a false light that was actually darkness. Every idea or experience of "peace" I had known previously was now revealed as the stillness of death rather than the true peace of life. I said, "Master, Teacher, I will do all that You wish. I surrender my life to You." From the very onset, I knew that my relationship with Him was directly related to obedience. To obey and surrender was also to abide in His presence. I knew what was happening to me had nothing to do with my efforts, but rather, was an act of divine kindness.

The wisps of clouds from the valley below swirled up the steep slopes. The sun splashed across the vast scene and a large and beautiful rainbow appeared. My life was never to be the same. An assurance, unlike any I had ever known, affirmed from within that I was finally on the true path. It became very clear to me that I was to follow Yeshua alone and depart from synthesizing philosophies and religions.

Heading toward Katmandu, I came across a small "airport." On each end of this dubious plateau airstrip were crumpled pieces of debris that were once small planes. Fortunately a flight was available. From the vantage point of that plane, what took many weeks of difficult walking could be seen at once. I could hardly believe I'd walked all the way. Upon my arrival at Katmandu, the Messiah said, "Go to the post office." It was mid-day and I really had no reason to go there. I entered the building and stood about for a moment. Suddenly, there appeared a familiar face: the missionary I'd met on the bus to Bhadgoan. Quickly, I exclaimed with joy my experience. He was astounded, and then heartily invited me to his dwelling. We ate and prayed and I was refreshed. He instructed me in basic matters with regard to this new path. After much prayer it seemed good to the both of us that I return to the United States.

The next few years of my life were devoted to the study of all of the Old and New Testaments. The entire experience was a profound process of cleansing and reorientation. Many hours and days were spent, totally engrossed in the revelation of God through his Word. Mighty clouds of confusion began to give way to the sunshine of truth. How great was the delusion that had captured my soul! Reincarnation, karma, astrology and the great blasphemous concept that man is inherently divine were completely washed from me.

The transformation of my life has been one of great joy. To be sure, there are still times of tribulation. But I can always enter the secret place that I have found in Messiah. There, in holy fellowship with Him, my heart drinks of life! It is true Life.

Commentary by Mike Shreve

Stanley's story captivates me—it amazes me—such hunger, such thirst for truth, and for the true God. His journey is a compelling illustration of a fulfilled promise God gave through a prophet long ago: *"You will seek Me and find Me, when you search for Me with ALL your heart"* (Jer. 29:13).

Very few people would endure such hardships for a glimpse of Ultimate Reality. Like many of the wandering sadhus of India, Stanley left the comforts of life behind to explore the supernatural realm. He was not disappointed, because God honors sincerity.

One of the most remarkable things about having a real encounter with the Lord Jesus is the transformation that takes place in the whole person. The Bible says we become a *"NEW CREATION."* Old things *"pass away"* and all things *"become new"* (2 Cor. 5:17). Everything changes: our attitudes, motivations, personality, spiritual condition, beliefs and destiny. The Bible even states that God puts a *"new spirit"* in us (Ezek. 36:26).

One of the strongest evidences of this dramatic change in Stanley's life was his final rejection of the "crown concept" of New Age philosophy: the idea that human beings are inherently divine. You may be wondering, "What's so wrong with the idea that we are all God?" To answer that, first, let's go to the "root" of the concept—*pantheism*.

This word *pantheism* comes from two Greek words: *pan*, which means "all" and *theos*, which means "God." So, according to this outlook: ALL IS GOD AND GOD IS ALL. Most eastern religions and

New Age mindsets are based on this concept, or something similar. The premise is that God did not "create" the universe (as something that exists apart from Him); but that God "emanated" the universe. Therefore, in this mindset, divinity is the core reality of everything. The Godhead (an impersonal force) veils "Itself" in the appearance of matter, but the physical world is really an illusion (the Hindus call it *maya*).

According to this perspective, everything is God—stars, planets, mountains, trees, flowers, horses, cats, dogs—everything! After reaching such an astounding conclusion, it's no quantum leap of logic to take the next step and conclude that we human beings are God also. How encouraging is that! How empowering! What could be wrong with such a confidence-building principle?

The big hang-up is that little two-letter word "we." If someone dares to boast that "*We* are God," that statement reaches out and embraces both the WORST of the human race (monsters like Adolph Hitler and Stalin) and the BEST of the human race (like Mahatma Gandhi or Mother Theresa). So both evil and good become expressions of God, both darkness and light are manifestations of Ultimate Reality. This is exactly what the yin-yang symbol of ancient Taoism represents (the two tear-drop shapes, one dark and the other light, inside a circle): that darkness and light are part of one complete whole. Please seriously consider the ramifications of the unavoidable conclusion:

If we attribute divinity to man, we must attribute sinfulness to God.

But the Bible clearly insists in the Old Testament, "*The Lord is upright...there is NO UNRIGHTEOUSNESS in Him*" (Ps. 92:15); and in the New Testament, "*God is light, and in Him is NO DARKNESS at all*" (1 John 1:5). These verses can only be true if biblical "theism" is the correct nature of the relationship between God and the universe: God existing apart from, or outside of, physical creation. In that scenario, the evil here in this world cannot be sourced in God. It must stream from other sources: first, satan and his demonic underlings, and second, the fallen nature of a human race that has willfully rebelled against the truth. God Himself is not the Author or Source of this evil; the free will He gave to angels and to humankind has allowed them to be the perpetrators of darkness in the universe.

The scenario of God being a mixture of good and evil should be totally unacceptable for any true lover of God—no matter how many gurus, swamis, psychics, Ascended Masters, or channeled spirits herald this concept as being right. Even the respected Hindu philosopher, Madhva, argued, "It is blasphemous to accept that a perfect God changes Himself into an imperfect world."[1] Pantheism blurs any distinction between God and people, to the point where some gurus even counsel against praying *to* God, because those who do so are making a highly contradictory statement. If *you* are God, why would you pray to *Yourself*?

In a true salvation experience, God fills us with Himself—so that we become *"partakers of the divine nature"* (filled with His wisdom, knowledge, power, joy and love)—but we never actually *become* God (2 Pet. 1:4). To claim that is the epitome of self-deception.

Endnote

1. "Dvaita," Miriam-Webster's Encyclopedia of World Religions (Springfield, MA: Merriam-Webster, Incorporated, 1999) p. 307.

About the Writer

Stanley Petrowski currently resides in a remote area of South-west Oregon with Alexandra, his wife of 34 years, doing the work of the Lord. They ranch organically and are very active in conservation issues of the region. They strive to live a simple life of prayer and study of the Word of God in anticipation of the Messiah's return.

Email: mohair@singingfalls.com

Website: www.singingfalls.com

Chapter 3

From Guru to God

By Michael Graham

*A follower of Swami Muktananda and
prominent teacher of the Avatar® Course
experiences true enlightenment!*

Interesting, spiritual things began for me with the "Three Bears" version of Christianity at a private boarding school operated by a mainline Christian denomination. With about 450 other students, for ten years, I had to attend 15 minutes of chapel five days a week, one and a half hours of chapel on Sundays, accompanied by big organ music, stained-glass windows, Kings James English, and a 20-minute mini-sermon. I don't think, after a decade, that a single boy understood who Jesus claimed to be and why He came. At the time, all we heard seemed a bit boring, really.

But around the age of 16, my brain woke up, and I started to reflect on life. All my friends seemed to know what they wanted to do when they left high school—go back on the farm, become a doctor, go into their dad's business or whatever—but I didn't have a clue what my interests were or what career I wanted to follow.

Stuck with this limitation, I began to read. My father was a doctor, a psychoanalyst, and something of a philosopher. Two books on the Eastern spiritual tradition, from the shelves of his big library, grabbed my attention: one on an Indian philosophy (Vedanta) and yoga, and the other on Buddhism. They promised a life free of suffering, personal transformation and an experience of the highest truth—Enlightenment. That was enough for me. Where do I sign?

After studying yoga and trying to learn how to meditate in Melbourne, Australia, for three years, I set off for India, the home of the mysteries of the East, the guru and every other marvelous thing. I embarked on a mission, at age 22, to find the truth and to be transformed.

After motorcycling throughout Sri Lanka and India, and taking a huge round through Pakistan, Afghanistan, and Iran and on through Europe to London, I returned to India to achieve my original purpose. I landed in the ashram of Swami Muktananda Paramahansa. He was a guru who later became famous in the West. He'd come to me on strong recommendation as one whose mere touch or presence could transform a person's life. As it turned out, I was his first Australian devotee.

The "Awakening"

Within a couple of days of my arrival at the ashram I had a private audience with Swami Muktananda. He was charismatic indeed, but only knew a few words of English. Through a translator, I told him that I had come to have my meditation fixed. All attempts to meditate successfully in Australia had failed. Instead of settling down into a quiet state, I'd become positively knotted up. He simply said, "Don't worry, everything will be fine."

A week passed, and I was meditating all alone in the meditation room, on a real tiger's skin. All of a sudden I was startled. Muktananda was standing over me. He stroked both cheeks, passed his palm over my forehead, turned on his heels and left. It took all of five seconds. "Well," I thought, "that was wonderful." The guru had touched me, and I knew that was supposed to be auspicious. Nothing happened at first, but a week later I wasn't to be disappointed.

This one afternoon, while meditating all alone, a strange phenomenon began. Suddenly while sitting, my body began to revolve in a circular motion. I thought to myself, "How interesting!" I'd stop it, and off it would go again. Up till this point whenever my body moved, it was I who moved it. With each minute that passed this movement grew stronger and stronger. I was delighted. I knew that I had received the "awakening" Muktananda was distinguished for being able to activate—the awakening of the *kundalini* or divine power within (known as the Serpent Power in the Eastern spiritual tradition). All the while I was in a cool state of mind, watching with fascination. No hypnosis, suggestion, or hysteria was involved.

This *kundalini* force is described as being "asleep" (like a coiled snake) until "awakened" through yogic disciplines over a lengthy period or more quickly through a guru's grace. The latter must be surrendered to since it is the spontaneous "grace-driven" means to self-realization—which was a most attractive concept to me back then. In the fullness of time one would be cleansed of all impurities that veiled the recognition of one's true identity being identical to the Supreme Reality—Brahman or "God."

Some days later, a Canadian chap turned up. We decided to go and meditate together. As we sat, he began to recite the famous Twenty-Third Psalm from the Bible:

The Lord is my Shepherd; I shall not want. He makes me to lie down in green pastures: He leads me beside the still waters. He restores my soul; He leads me in the paths of righteousness for His name's sake. Yea, though I walk through the valley of death I will fear no evil, for You are with me; Your rod and Your staff, they comfort me. You prepare a table before me in the presence of my enemies. You anoint my head with oil; my cup runs over. Surely goodness and mercy will follow me all the days of my life, and I will dwell in the house of the Lord forever.

I remembered that pleasant Bible passage from the light Christian enculturation during my schoolboy days. Suddenly, the "awakening" that had begun a few days before exploded into ten times its power. I was flung to the floor and started crawling my way along, growling like a lion, with the strength of ten men coursing through me. It was not as any ham actor could do; it was devastatingly real.

I was agog, watching it happen with amazement. I was not afraid. And I didn't resist it, since that wouldn't have been the idea. The poor Canadian chap had never seen anything like it. He commented later that the nearest thing he'd seen to it was an LSD drug freak-out; but this was something else! He was scared out of his wits and tried to settle down the situation by repeating the mantra, *Guru Om, Guru Om*, over and over out loud.

From that day on, whenever I gave over to the "awakening," there was continuous spontaneous activity. There were powerful breathing rhythms (*pranayama*), movement into classic dance formations, vigorously executed yoga-like postures, utterances like the sound of different birds, speaking in an unknown language, weeping bitterly in one second then laughing loudly in the next with nothing to weep or laugh about, cross-legged hopping across the ground like a frog, intense shaking of the body, classical hand gestures (*mudras*), the seeing of inner lights, journeys out of the body and innumerable other experiences.

It wasn't as though I was tuning in to some impulse to move in a certain way and going with it, as in psychodrama. It just grabbed me in a powerful, nonvolitional or spontaneous manner and moved me about. And there were moments of "dynamic" stillness. The predominantly physical manifestations are called *kriyas* in the Sanskrit language. Though at the time I felt these were a genuine expression of that internal "divine life," now I hold to a different perspective.

The Ashram Routine

All this was set into a typical Eastern framework of thinking. Muktananda would say, "God dwells within you as you"—the inner self or Brahman or God were identical. Spiritual practice consisted of faith in the guru as the self-realized master. It required surrender to his person and to his instructions, singing chants in the ancient Sanskrit language to the guru's glory, and devotional service. Its purpose was spiritual purification leading to the experience of one's own divinity, called self-realization, or enlightenment.

This particular path was called *siddha yoga*; the word *siddha* meaning "perfected being," and *yoga* meaning, "yoked to God," or *supreme reality*. So this was the union with God that was to take place through the grace of the perfected Master.

It sounded like an appealing truth. It was promising. It had an engine that moved things. So I stayed on in the ashram for five and a half months, participating in the rigorous daily routine. We'd arise at four in the morning for 90 minutes of meditation. If you were fortunate enough to receive the "awakening," you'd surrender to its workings as a dispassionate witness. If it had yet to stir in you, you'd sit in formal meditation repeating the Guru's mantra, *Soham,* meaning, "He I am" or "I am God," in the hope that it would happen soon.

That was the understanding in those days. However, instructions changed over the years. Then we took a cup of chai: sweet, spicy Indian tea. This was followed by 90 minutes of chanting the most famous Hindu scripture, *The Bhagavad Gita*. Then we were off into the beautiful gardens or marble courtyard to do a couple of hours work, a form of devotional service to the Guru, followed by 30 minutes of chanting the mantra, *Om Namah Shivaya* (meaning, "I bow to Shiva"—one of the chief gods in the Hindu pantheon).

Next came lunch—I called it "Hindu army chow"—simple and delicious. Then there was a one-hour voluntary chant, followed by another two hours of work, then a time called *dharshan*, when the guru would come out into a beautiful marble courtyard to be gazed upon or greeted, and then 45 minutes of meditation before dinner. Finally, a 60-minute chant was sung before we collapsed into bed at nine at night. Phew! Not a routine for the faint-hearted. This went seven days a week, 365 days a year. It was like something you might find in an eleventh-century Benedictine monastery.

This path of spirituality became my core spiritual practice for the next 16 years. I returned to India many times. I spent a total of four years in the country. But despite all the amazing spiritual experiences, signs, and wonders (including *nirvana*, a complete, but temporary annihilation of identity and sense of self, and the Hindu state of enlightenment called *turiya*), my deepest hopes for inner fulfillment remained unmet. The dynamism and apparent intelligence of the "awakening" particularly drew me in and kept me hopeful for future transformation. At the same time, I had been casting around for supplementary means to add to this Eastern practice that might have opened a crack to the light for which I was looking.

Self-help Programs

So, in the 1970s, 1980s, and 1990s, I did a number of the leading-edge personal development programs of the day: Landmark Education, once called EST, then Forum: a sort of no-nonsense, pragmatic, spiritual boot camp; and Silva Mind Control, a get-down-into-low-brain-wave-process, heal-people, throw-open-some-doors-of-psychic-perception, and reprogram-yourself-for-success type of program.

Then there was The Hoffman Quadrinity Process, an expe..
turbo-expunging of impeding, parent-induced, past psychological
impressions.

Then I studied and practiced *A Course in Miracles*: a well-developed
argument for spiritual transcendence, which I buried into for a year
with great discipline. I was intrigued by the observation that even
though I understood and believed the course's content, I continued to
think, feel, act and perform as though I'd never heard of it. My friends
on this course had the same experience. I was starting to discover that
the merely mental or cognitive approach to transformation is impo-
tent to do anything much.

I saw a gain here and there from a number of these courses. Whenever I was exposed to a new perspective, information, data or technique, there would be a slight shift, just enough to lead to an increase
of interest. Then there would be a plateau, a falling off, then a "What's
next?" Within days there was always a leak-back to the old familiar
self. This stuff wasn't delivering on its promise. I wasn't a dilettante. I
usually drilled down close to the bottom of these things, enough to see
whether I was dealing with iron pyrites (fool's gold) or something more
substantial. My basic Siddha Yoga practice kept on as the mainstay.

In 1982 Swami Muktananda died. Shortly afterward, I became one
of the ashram managers in India. Following this, for one tour, I fell
into the role of being an international tour manager of one of his suc-
cessors, the young Swami Nityananda. Months after I left this work, a
coup took place. Gurumayi, his sister and co-successor, ousted him for
behavior unbecoming to a guru. The whole affair unfolded like a palace
intrigue—something like Shakespeare could have written about.

At this time, I was in New York and got a call from an Australian
friend who'd just landed a huge Corporate Cultural Change contract
with Australia's second-largest company, Telecom Australia. He
invited me Down Under. Together with a team of five others, we put

together a broad range of personal and organizational development strategies designed to set Telecom up for success in an emerging, competitive, telecommunications marketplace. We believe it was the biggest corporate program of its type undertaken in the Southern Hemisphere.

By now, I'd had a broad and deep experience of the Eastern "Old Age" movement out of India, the pragmatic world of corporate consulting and the "New Age" personal development trainings.

Further, in 1988 I spotted this program called Avatar, created by a fellow called Harry Palmer. It was a belief management program, not dissimilar in theory to what we'd taught corporately. But this guy claimed that he had the techniques that could really make the difference. Up until then, I had found that core beliefs were not amenable to change. This was a "create your preferred reality" program—beliefs are real forces; they determine the way you think, feel, behave, and perform. Change your beliefs and thereby change your life!

So I jumped on a plane for Los Angeles and found myself in the home of Marilyn Ferguson, author of the million-copy, best-seller book *The Aquarian Conspiracy*. She was a participant, along with me and nine others. It was an expensive course at $2,000. It included tea and biscuits, but no meals or accommodations. It went for four or five days. How interesting; one of the facilitators was Ingo Swann, a man I'd heard had the most accurate strike rate among psychics tested by Stanford University under controlled conditions. He'd been their research subject for 16 years and later worked 12 years for the United States Central Intelligence Agency (CIA) experimenting with procedures of remote viewing (visual perception beyond the range of bodily senses). I got to know Ingo well and stayed with him in New York City. He was teaching this course quite independently of his psychic abilities. He's no longer associated with Avatar.

Teaching the Avatar Course

The course was more powerful than most. I was sufficiently impressed to fly to New York and spend another $3,000 for nine days of training so I could deliver the program under license. I became one of the more successful teachers of Avatar around the world, delivering the program in Australia, New Zealand, Singapore, Switzerland, United States, and Canada. Beyond this, I delivered my own program, the Decision Principle Training*, in France as well. It proposes decision as the first principle of existence. Palmer's top Avatar course was called Wizards*. Held over nine days and at $7,500, it promised the dominion of the gods. It didn't deliver. Again, as with previous courses, the substance wasn't to the level expected. However, throughout all these years I kept meditating.

By now, I had many years of experience, thousands of hours of meditation, supernatural phenomena, study, and the company of spiritual luminaries. So I do believe my walk was characterized by a considerable degree of discipline and application, and all this wasn't too much to cover over a 28-year span.

By providence, I had arrived at the doorsteps of famous spiritual luminaries before most people in the West had heard of them. To name only a few: Swami Muktananda, my guru, who later became guru to famous singer John Denver; and there was Osho (Rajneesh), the famous or infamous Indian guru, owner of 93 Rolls Royce cars, and founder of the "Orange People," who made world news for themselves in Oregon; and Sathya Sai Baba, the guru with the largest following in the world. Then there were the works and the company of the Christian, Islamic and Buddhist mystics, such as the Tibetan Buddhist Chogyam Trungpa.

Over the years I observed that people had different motives for following a guru or getting involved in such groups. Some sought personal development or victory over personal limitations. I was partially motivated by this. Some sought community; for others, it was a life-style choice. Some wanted position and power. Others wanted to be loved. Yet others were spiritual hedonists, thirsting for the next experiential high. Being looked after was a priority for some. The search for meaning may have been high among the reasons. In most people, motives were probably mixed, and not thoroughly reflected upon. Very few, I believe, were actually trying to divide the wheat from the chaff (distinguish truth from falsehood). Two primary things were of profound interest to me: first, what practice or belief system could actually make a difference; and second, what was actually true among all these theories.

The Buddha repudiated the teachings of the Hindu scriptures. Famous Hindu masters repudiated the Buddha's teaching, putting a dent in Buddhism on the Indian subcontinent from which it never recovered. Without going into detail here, contradictions between teachings abounded.

I noticed that many of my friends tended to swallow all they were told, hook-line-and-sinker, without much reflective assessment. Often, superstition just took over. Truth mattered when it came to balancing a checkbook, but in matters of spirituality, well, anything went.

With all this under my belt—exposure to luminaries, powerful spiritual experiences, and the understanding I'd developed—I still believed that breaking through the Gates of Heaven in a sustainable way was possible. I took what I had been given in personal revelation and the best of what I had been exposed to, and put it all together, calling it *The Reality Training*. I fully believed this amalgam of practices would build the momentum for breakthrough. My life had really become a serious experiment, with encounters and spiritual experiences spurring me on. Perhaps I was like a bloodhound following a scent.

At this point, I decided to go into isolation. Since my late teens, I thought this would make an interesting experiment and had never had the chance to do it. Now was the time. At the back of my home was a tiny apartment. I asked an accommodating friend to fashion wooden panels to cover the windows and a trap door through which food could be passed. I was sealed up in this way, and spent ten days in there. Great! I came out on a Monday and it was as though, through new eyes, the world sparkled. By Tuesday the old familiar perception had returned.

The Turning Point

Seeing potential in this experiment, I repeated it some time later. On the second day, a remarkable event took place. I was just settling myself onto a couch. I was in a completely ordinary state of mind— no meditation, no spiritual preparation—yet something quite over-whelming happened. The image of Jesus Christ formed up within my chest cavity. With this image came the conviction of who He was. One second following, there was an experience beyond all words can tell. If I were to step it down into the poverty of language, there was an open-ness and love coming from Jesus to me of cosmic proportions and an invitation. It was as if He was saying, "Give me your life and breath and I'll take care of you."

Well, I was staggered, amazed, delighted all at once. The unique feature of this love was that it was communicated to me to an ulti-mate degree. It was utterly real and personal, but I didn't know how to respond. I was so committed to the Eastern-oriented practice that I kept doing precisely that. This encounter, however, I could never forget.

A year passed and I'd gone to Berkeley, California, to conduct intro-ductory programs for The Reality Training I'd created. Here, a second significant event took place. Over a three-day period, as if pressed into me from outside myself, came the conviction that everything I had done, the thousands of hours of meditation, the realizations and spiritual experiences, had all added up to a *huge fat zero*. A 28-year investment just tipped over. It felt as though I'd been trying to draw water from an empty well. Wow! I was sobered. "Well," I thought, "I'll just run plum ordinary now, become a regular meat-and-potatoes guy, and live out my span and do what I can. Simple."

However, at the time I was doing a 25-minute drive in the car to Marin County near San Francisco, each day. I kept catching these evangelical preachers on the radio teaching the historic faith from the Bible. They were good speakers. It was a bit interesting, and besides, I was interested in the five Great Traditions (unlike the cults) that had stood the test of time—Hinduism, Buddhism, Islam, Judaism, and Christianity. So, here was Christianity being explained better than I'd heard it before, at least the biblically oriented form of it.

At first, I was noticing the similarities between elements of the Eastern and Christian worldviews; then it became the *differences* that got my attention. Listening to the broadcasts themselves, plus sending away for the tapes advertised on the radio over the next few months, I must have logged about 150 hours of Jesus-centered, biblical teaching.

With still no contact with followers of Jesus, I was being educated to the first principles of Christianity. I noted the claims Jesus made for Himself: His claim to deity, His purpose for coming. I learned to appreciate what He accomplished by His death on the cross (taking upon Himself all the sins that could have eternally separated us from God) and His resurrection from the dead (giving us hope that we, too, will one day receive resurrected bodies at the coming of the Lord). Remembering my personal encounter with Him, and having been reduced to nothing anyway, with nothing to lose, I resolved to acknowledge Jesus Christ as my Lord and Savior. Yikes! Those words seemed uncomfortably religious to me at the time. Too bad, I was going ahead anyway.

This was going to be the most important decision I'd ever made. I knew about decision: its power, place, and importance. I'd taught my Decision Principle* Training around the world. I could have made the decision in my living room, but I wanted to make a marker of this one. I saw a billboard promoting Billy Graham coming to town. I'd heard of him—the twentieth century's most famous evangelist. "What a perfect opportunity to make a decision in front of thousands of witnesses," I thought to myself.

It was September 1997. With considerable anticipation, I awaited the day of his arrival. At the appointed hour, I was one the first ones at the stadium and mounted the stands. He talked. When he invited people down to make that decision to receive Jesus as their Savior, down I went. I was so close to the podium, I could have reached up and almost polished his shoes. When the moment came to decide, I made that decision, surely, definitely, no turning back.

I was never the same again. It happened silently, un-dramatically. I knew what it meant to be born again, that strange phrase. Something new began in me that moment. A peace came over me. With it came new meaning and purpose and, above all, a substantive change of heart and mind. This "change" had eluded me throughout all those years of experience, meditation practice, and yogic phenomena. And this had come as a pure gift of grace, independent of all my efforts, disciplines, or practice.

New Understanding

What do I mean by a change of heart and mind? Well, my temperament or disposition started to soften, among other characteristics. I noticed it; my son noticed it. That was good enough for me. The seeker had died. I'd come to rest. Perhaps I could have used terms like that in the past, but no, this was new coin.

So, here I was, having found my sufficiency in Christ—no supplementation required. In Him are *hidden all the treasures of wisdom and knowledge,* as the Bible states (Col. 2:3).

tude toward the concept of God significantly changed: ...wed and made proper. Paul's description of Jesus to the Christians in Colosse struck me hard:

He is the image of the invisible God, the firstborn over all creation. For by Him all things were created that are in heaven and that are on earth, visible and invisible, whether thrones or dominions or principalities or powers. All things were created by Him and for Him. And He is before all things, and in Him all things consist (Colossians 1:15-17).

Ironically, it made sense to know the biblical view, that I was not God or the supreme self, even in essence (Hinduism, Advaita Vedanta); or self "blown out," as in nirvana (Buddhism), but a creature created by God in His image and likeness, fashioned for eternal relationship with Him. This seemed like a truth free of all vestiges of cosmic narcissism.

The Bible came alive to me with a quality and a texture unlike other written works of an intellectual or spiritual nature. It became to me like sweet milk and meat to the soul. This didn't mean I had to like everything it said. Nevertheless, I believed it. The adjustment had to be mine. I was no longer on the throne as arbiter of all truth. This was quite a leap, and as I came to observe later, becomes a mark of someone who has enjoyed a genuine conversion.

So here I was, reading the Bible with new eyes, spending time in prayer, listening to excellent preaching and enjoying church fellowship. What a change! This was a U-turn that I would have never believed possible. It was a genuine and radical turnaround—a turnaround at the root. Nothing else but the Holy Spirit, not the spirit of the *kundalini*, nor the spirit of the guru, could have penetrated to the core of my ruin: a ruin that I believe everyone shares.

What was the fruit of the Messiah's grace? Rest—a rest pertaining to my existence, most assuredly superior to passing minutes of stillness or peace I may have experienced in meditation. I have come to appreciate that this new life is something Jesus wants for *everyone,* irrespective of race or religion. It is a *unique* and eternal boon available to everyone who turns to Him with confidence.

So, today I walk on in gratitude. With a thorough basis for comparison, I cannot but hold to the preeminence and supremacy of Jesus Christ and His marvelous grace. Yes, His promises and declarations have captivated me, such as the following:

"Apart from Me you can do nothing" (John 15:5 NIV).

"Come to Me, all of you who are weary and loaded down with burdens, and I will give you rest" (Matthew 11:29 ISV).

"I am the Way, the Truth and the Life. No one comes to the Father except through Me" (John 14:6).

"I am the light of the world. He who follows Me shall not walk in darkness..." (John 8:12).

"Whoever drinks the water I shall give him...will become in him a fountain of water springing up into everlasting life" (John 4:14).

"Behold, I stand at the door, and knock. If anyone hears My voice, and opens the door, I will come in to him, and dine with him, and he with Me" (Revelation 3:20).

These promises and invitations have beckoned me. Perhaps they are beckoning you now.

The general "God" word was big in the early days of my search, as it is today, yet Jesus Christ pointed to Himself as having a *special* saving relationship to the world. It became clear to me, as I combed these notions thoroughly, that He wasn't speaking of the popular New Age concept of the Christ consciousness, or any other contemporary, fashionable, or mystic view. Rather, He revealed Himself to me as the once historic and now ever-present, eternal figure of Jesus Christ, who is *"the same yesterday, today and forever"* (Hebrews 13:8). It is this Jesus I present to you.

Commentary by Mike Shreve

Michael Graham was certainly not a novice in the practices and beliefs of Far Eastern mysticism. He maintained a consistent level of self-discipline and commitment to his path for nearly three decades—before turning his heart toward the cross of Calvary. This, in itself, should stir other seekers of truth to stop and take notice.

A major spiritual milestone in Michael's life was the alleged "awakening" of the kundalini (the Serpent Power) he received through Swami Muktananda (an impartation called *shaktipat).* A supernatural power definitely manifested, but the big questions are: "Was it a true experience of God?" and "If not, where did the power come from?" (You may want to do some research on the symbolism of the serpent found in the Bible—Genesis 3:1-14, Revelation 12:14-15, 20:2.)

Traditional Far Eastern/New Age teaching asserts the kundalini is the "essence of divine life" that resides within every human being—so to discover God, seekers are taught to look within. True Christian belief does not agree with this view. Instead, the Scripture states that we have actually been *"separated"* from God because of our sins (Isa. 59:2). So prior to the experience of union with God, the Creator is external, not internal.

The birth of the Church on the Day of Pentecost verifies this perspective. When the 120 disciples in the upper room had their amazing supernatural encounter with God, it was not a "Serpent Power" awakened *within* them. It was the power of God entering *into* them. The divine presence came into that gathering with a sound like a *"rushing mighty wind... and they were all FILLED with the Holy Spirit."* (Acts 2:2-4). Yes, the Most High came *into* them from *outside* of them. At that precise moment, they came into oneness with a personal Creator, not an impersonal life force. They entered a relationship *with* God; they did not consciously *become* God. The difference between these two perspectives is huge.

Another major point—when I studied yoga, I often heard gurus and teachers warn against a "premature arousal" of the kundalini. They cautioned if a devotee did not sufficiently prepare for this experience through intense yogic disciplines, an awakening could result in very negative things, like the manifestation of dark psychic powers, encounters with demonic beings, insanity, or even death.

Notably, there is absolutely no account in the Bible of a true experience of God causing such dark and dreadful results. Much the opposite, it delivers from evil, frees the heart from darkness, grants power over demonic forces, imparts *"a sound mind"* and confers the wondrous gift of *"everlasting life"* (2 Tim. 1:7, John 3:16). God is only good, so a true encounter with Him can only bring forth good results. Therefore, any experience that can potentially produce destructive results must come from another source, from the realm of darkness and not from the light.

What about this supposed need for spiritual preparation? I have personally seen thousands of people come to the Lord *directly* out of a life of sin and rebellion. It wasn't necessary for them to go through years of spiritual disciplines before it was *safe* for them to experience spiritual rebirth. It just took a momentary decision and a simple request, asking Jesus into their hearts to be Lord of their lives. That's all it will take for you.

At one point in his spiritual journey, Michael studied *A Course in Miracles*. In that book, author Helen Schucman emphasizes having correct, loving attitudes toward fellow human beings, which is certainly helpful and admirable. However, she asserts that "salvation is nothing more than right-mindedness" and that "the crucifixion had no part in the atonement."[1] She also taught that "it is impossible to think of anything" God "created that could need forgiveness."[2] Yet these are essential aspects of the transformation available through Jesus, our Messiah. We *do* need forgiveness from God, and the cross *is* central to that occurring. It is not enough to just become a good person with a good heart toward others. We need to be cleansed. Jesus taught that when we pray, we should request, *"Father... forgive us our sins"* (Luke 11:2-4). Right-mindedness necessarily includes understanding how to access that forgiveness.

All it takes is humility, repentance, and faith. God is ready and willing to respond. You can experience it now. Just put yourself in a receptive mode. JESUS is ready to fill you with his great love and give you *a new beginning and a new heart!* The promise is clear—*"Ask and it will be given to you"* (Luke 11:9).

Endnotes

1. Helen Schucman and William Thetford, A Course in Miracles (Tiburon, CA: Foundation for Inner Peace, 1976), "Text," pp. 53, 264.

2. Ibid., "Manual For Teachers," p. 79.

About the Writer

Michael Graham is a corporate consultant specializing in corporate cultural change. He currently delivers the Decision Principle Training®. An ordained Baptist pastor, he also speaks on Hinduism, Buddhism, and the "new" contemporary spirituality, contrasting them to true, biblical Christianity. He has appeared as a guest speaker on television and radio and divides his time between the United States, South Asia, and Australia. He has authored a full-length book on his amazing, 28-year spiritual odyssey titled, *From Guru to God: The Experience of Ultimate Truth*.

Email: youturnworks@gmail.com

Website: www.youturnworks.com

Chapter 4

From Death to Life

By Sid Roth

A consulter of psychics and mind control practitioner receives amazing counsel from the Source of all wisdom!

My God! How had anyone been able to stand me? Why hadn't somebody killed me long before now? I didn't like the sudden blinding revelation that showed me to myself—the revelation that I, who had always thought I was so wonderful, was a total washout as a person. It sickened. It hurt. I wanted to deny it, but try as I might I couldn't think of one justification for my life. There wasn't a single good, decent quality in me. Why was God letting me live?

Maybe He wasn't! The thought careened through my head, and I couldn't stop it. Maybe the flashing of my whole life before me was a prelude to its end…that very day. But God! I'm not ready to die!

I drove aimlessly around the city for several hours going like an automaton through the mechanical motions of stopping for traffic signals, changing lanes, accelerating, slowing, thinking....

As I considered the life I'd lived, really seeing myself for the first time, the evil that was in me seemed to swell larger and larger, until I feared I would burst with it. But why? Why had I been like that? Why had I never seen it until now? Was there any hope for me?

As the unanswerable questions swirled, I considered crashing my car into the fast-moving traffic to wipe out the awfulness of the past. But I was afraid. If I did that, maybe I would land in hell, stuck with my own awfulness for an unending forever.

Unexplainably, I found myself parking in front of a big bookstore I had frequented in the past. As I entered the store, my feet took me automatically down the aisle to the New Age section. There, a book with a blue jacket leaped out at me—*The Bible, the Supernatural, and the Jews* by McCandlish Phillips. I reached for it, it fell open in my hands, and I began to read:

> If you would not thrust your hand into a snake pit, you should not permit yourself to be drawn into an involvement with one or another form of occultism, even in a tentative and experimental way, without knowing that it is possible for you to step over a threshold and past a door that will slam shut behind you as soon as you stand on the far side of it— slam shut so tight that nothing you can do can ever get that door open again so that you can get back out.[1]

Had the door already slammed shut on me because of my involvement with horoscopes, fortune-telling, and mind control? My heart was beating wildly as my eyes skipped through the pages a little further. There I read something even more terrifying:

> The door that can never be opened again slams shut faster on a Jew than on a non-Jew.[2]

The author went on to say that this is true because every Jew, whether he knows it or not, is in a covenant relationship with God.

I felt beads of sweat popping out on my forehead. My throat was on fire. The gooseflesh of fear enveloped my whole body. But I couldn't put the book down. I shoved some money across the counter to the checkout clerk and dashed back to my car, the book tightly clenched under my arm. I wasn't even aware of driving to the apartment, just of suddenly arriving there, slamming the door of the car, and dashing through the lobby and into my room, torn with warring desires. Part of me wanted to devour the book, to read every word; another part of me wanted to rip it to shreds, to set it on fire—anything to get rid of it!

The page to which I opened named prominent Jews who had lost their lives because they had dabbled in the occult, opening the door to the supernatural through acid rock music, alcohol, marijuana, drugs, yoga, martial arts, meditation, channeling, séances, psychic healing, acupuncture, hypnotism, and mind expansion. There was Brian Epstein, manager of the Beatles. Brian, a multimillionaire at 30—he was a Jew. He had dabbled in the occult, and died of an overdose of drugs. I shuddered, thinking how close I had come to following in his footsteps exactly. But I didn't want to die! I wasn't ready to die!

Oh God, help me! Somebody, help me!

I had to get in touch with God! I had to tell Him how sorry I was. For everything.

But I didn't know how to get in touch with God, and I didn't know who could help me. My fortune-teller couldn't help me. The mind control people couldn't help me. They said there was no such thing as evil. My rabbi? He'd probably send me to a psychiatrist who would lock me up and throw the key away. My mother couldn't help me. She didn't know how to reach God, either.

Panic stricken, I rushed out and ran to a jewelry store in the neighborhood. There I bought a *mezuzah*3 and hung it around my neck.

Maybe that would show God that I belonged to Him. I telephoned Joy, my estranged wife.

"Pray for me," I pleaded. "Pray like you've never prayed before! Pray to your God for me! Ask Him to help me. *Please* ask Him to help me. Ask Him to spare my life!" I let the phone fall from my hand, weeping in an agony of despair.

I could feel the fear building in me, a tangible thing building toward a crescendo. When the crash came, where would I be? Or would there be anything left of me to be anywhere?

Feeling like a man under a death sentence, I put a Bible under my pillow, touched the *mezuzah* around my neck, and crawled, trembling, into bed. Lying there on my back, rigid with terror, I cried out to God for help. It wasn't much of a prayer, but it came from a broken, empty man.

Before I tell you how I found a solution, I need to show you how I got to this pivotal place in my life...

Bad Choices

Years before, in my effort to obtain instant riches, I "invested" $2,600 in a sure-fire scheme with someone who turned out to be a con artist. Needless to say, I never saw the money again. But I was on my way to make a million, and $2,600 was less than a drop in the bucket. My wife, Joy, finally quit bugging me about it. I guess she felt that I had suffered enough. Mom kept building me up by talking about what an awful cruel man my ex-friend had been to bilk me of our savings in that way.

My own indignation was used up, my wounds began to heal, and my eternal optimism took over. Having just moved back to my hometown of Washington, D.C., I poured myself back into the role of becoming a millionaire in a hurry by selling life insurance.

My first year in life insurance I wound up with policies worth almost a million dollars in force. I was doing so well that Joy quit her hated secretarial job and went back to school full time to learn to be an interior designer. We had moved into our own apartment, a great relief to both of us after having been cooped up with Joy's parents for two months. We almost felt we were happy together again. But it wasn't real, and it didn't last. Soon we were back in our respective roles of merely tolerating one another's presence.

One day, my Uncle Abe called, all excited about a new kind of life insurance policy that was tied in with a mutual fund. It sounded different all right, but lousy. I told him so, and insisted that what I was selling was far superior to what anyone else had to offer. I knew that Uncle Abe had my best interests at heart, however, and I agreed to meet with him and the other agent and hear about the other guy's "superior" product.

Much to my surprise, after two hours, I agreed that his product was better than mine, and I was ready to change jobs. When I told my boss I was quitting, he was furious, because not only was I quitting, I was taking two of the best salesmen on his force with me into the new thing.

"Sid, you can't do that!" He roared. "It's against every rule of ethics! We paid to move you up here, and we've got a big investment in you and those other salesmen. We're entitled to a return on our investment!" The louder he shouted, the more right he was, the more immovable I became.

"Look," I told him, a menacing tone in my voice, "I've already contributed more than enough to this outfit. I'd be a fool not to put my own best interests first, and that goes for these other guys, too. You don't own us, you know."

After the sneering way I talked to him, it's a wonder he didn't throw me out.

During my second year in the insurance business, this time with Chatfield Associates, I sold over a million dollars worth of insurance again. By the end of the year, I was a manager with ten men under me. My sales unit was one of the top production units in the country, and hardly a week passed without a telegram congratulating me for some new sales achievement.

Somewhere along the line, after about a year and a half with Chatfield, it occurred to me that if I could sell so well for other people, I was a fool to line their pockets. I ought to move out on my own, start my own company, and then I'd really be bringing it in.

But my own company wasn't doing well. Something seemed to go wrong with my selling ability, and I wasn't able to communicate it to the men I hired to work for me. The office moved too slowly, and after less than six months, I closed up shop and took a new position with another outfit. For part of a year, I worked for them as a regional manager, traveling a lot, setting up offices, and training personnel. But it went sour, too. I recognized that I was going nowhere fast, and I began looking for another position, one where they would really appreciate me. In spite of my initial success in selling life insurance, all I wanted was out.

In the midst of my job-hopping, Joy told me that we were expecting a baby. Well!

After our daughter was born, even I could see that hopping from one poorly done job to another was no way to raise a family. When I was given a chance to go to work as an executive with Merrill, Lynch, Pierce, Fenner, and Smith, one of the finest investment companies in America, I recognized it as being exactly what I needed. No more peddling life insurance. Any clod could do that. This was the career spot I should have been in years ago. The sky was the limit.

Separation

After three months of local training, I went to New York for more intensive instruction. During the two months I spent there, away from

Joy and our baby girl, I made the rounds of the singles' bars at night. I turned into a real swinger. Whatever shreds of our marriage had been left hanging together disintegrated completely.

Not because I wanted to, but out of a peculiar obedience to some kind of *ought to,* I telephoned Joy from a bar on New Year's Eve. She was crying when she answered the phone, but she managed to sob out that her father, who had been an alcoholic for years, had just shot himself in the head.

Joy sounded so pitiful, so alone, so upset, that I got a cab to the airport and was on the next plane for Washington. But where I had been and what I had become were so sickeningly obvious to Joy when she saw me that she told me I needn't have bothered to come home. Our marriage was finished.

Joy had endured all the unfaithfulness, all the neglect she could take from me. She wanted just one thing more. A separation.

Separation. Unthinkable for a Jewish family. When I was a child, my parents had talked seriously of separation once. My father had said that he and I would move to New York, and Shirley would stay in Washington with Mom. He promised that I'd love it in New York with him, but I couldn't imagine life without Mom fighting my battles for me, and I couldn't imagine Dad living without her, either, no matter how violently they disagreed about some things.

Somehow they had worked out their differences or figured how to live with them, and the split hadn't happened. As I examined my own feelings, I admitted that a part of me wanted to leave Joy all right, but there was another part that seemed to want us to stay together in spite of everything. It was going to be a difficult decision for me to make.

Hooked

For the last two years, I had been turning to a fortune-teller for help with the major decisions in my life. I would ask him what I should do.

Truth Seekers

For as long as I could remember, I had been interested in everything to do with the New Age, occult, astrology, fortune-telling, handwriting analysis, reincarnation, hypnosis, communicating with the dead, spiritualism, Ouija boards, and psychic powers. All held a fascination for me that was far beyond a mere hobby or fad or interest. It was as if a supernatural force drew me, and when one of my mother's friends had told her one day about the new fortune-teller she'd discovered and how positively fantastic he was, I was quick to get his address.

When I first went into the nondescript office building where he had his place of business, I found the fortune-teller himself to be a very solid, ruddy-faced individual instead of the wraith the atmosphere of the place suggested. He was sitting behind a screen in the corner of a shabby room that served also as a waiting area for his clients, and I seated myself across the rickety card table from him. The first thing he told me as he shuffled through his cards and fanned them out sent chills down my spine.

"Sir, your parents live near Sixteenth Street in upper Northwest near Kennedy Street," he said matter-of-factly.

Wow! How could he have known that? They lived just one block from Kennedy! That was near all right. And there was no way he could have known that just from looking at me.

I was so impressed with the fortune-teller's supernatural knowledge that I consulted him about every major decision from then on. Several times, Joy and I quarreled over the fact that I couldn't seem to decide anything without consulting him first. There were periods when I visited him several times a week.

Once it occurred to me to wonder, since he had such supernatural powers, why he wasn't a millionaire in the stock market, why he didn't have a plusher office, why he needed my miserable three dollars a visit. But I quickly brushed such questioning aside. I was hooked.

When I asked the fortune-teller whether or not I should leave Joy, he gave me a strong go-ahead, and I was relieved that I didn't have to make the decision for myself.

Looking in the newspaper for a place to stay, I found a roommate referral service that put me in touch with a swinging bachelor named Jeff. His apartment was nicely furnished, immaculately clean. There was only one catch. Jeff's girlfriend shared his bedroom.

"Sid, do you mind if my girlfriend sleeps with me?" He asked. "Yes," I answered. "I do mind—because she isn't sleeping with me." We laughed, and I had passed the test.

When Joy was at work the next day, I moved my clothes out of our apartment and drove off into my new, exciting, glamorous, bachelor-at-large life. Wanting to make a clean break with everything in my past, I asked the fortune-teller if it would be all right for me to change jobs again. He had always approved my job changes before, even triggered my looking for a new job sometimes by telling me that I would be changing jobs soon, but this time he turned thumbs down, advising me against leaving Merrill Lynch. He had an elderly client who sold stocks from time to time and gave the money to him. I was a convenient broker to handle these transactions without asking foolish questions.

Still, I knew I wasn't measuring up at Merrill Lynch, and it would be easier to start over somewhere else than to dig in and do a good job there. I didn't take the fortune-teller's advice but jumped when a new company offered me a stock option for going with them.

Having failed to take the fortune-teller's advice I decided not to see him again, but I felt absolutely lost without someone to turn to for guidance.

Power Hook-Up

One day, Mike Wasserman, my assistant sales manager at Glenwood Equities, my new job, was talking to me about one of his cases.

He knew I had consulted a fortune-teller in the past, and he started telling me about a friend of his who once had no fortune-telling ability of his own at all, but who had taken a mind-control course that revolutionized his life. Now he had supernatural abilities far beyond those of any ordinary fortune-teller. He knew things about other people that he had no natural way of knowing; he knew what was going to happen in the future; he knew everything he needed to know.

Wow! That sounded like exactly what I needed. I could no longer hide the fact that my ability in business was getting shaky. My sales had no staying power, and I was losing clients right and left. My best salesmen were leaving me. All in all, I had hit a real string of bad luck. If I had some of the psychic ability Mike's friend had received from the mind-control course, maybe then I could stay on top of things. Why, with that kind of ability, I probably wouldn't even need a job!

On my next Saturday off, I drove up to New Jersey to meet Mike's friend to give him an acid test. "Russ," I said, getting right to the point of my visit, "your friend Mike has been telling me that the mind-control course you took enables you to tap into supernatural power so you know things you have no natural way of knowing. Is that right?"

"Try me," he challenged. "See for yourself. Just give me the name of someone who's had something wrong with him, and I will tell you what it is. Anyone at all." "Gilmore Young," I said, giving him the name of Joy's father. Russ closed his eyes, seemed to be concentrating intently, his eyelids fluttering, and said, "I see a light starting toward this man—toward his head. It's entering his head...and starting to shatter..."

Russ's eyes popped wide with wonder as he stammered, "Could this man have been shot in his head...with a bullet?" That was all I needed to know. Russ had supernatural power all right. Just think what I could do when that power was mine!

90

A new mind-control class would begin in the DC area in a month. I marked it on my calendar, crossing off the days as it came closer and closer. I knew it would be what I had been searching for all my life, a can't-fail approach to acclaim and financial success.

If I could have known that what lay ahead was not acclaim and success but stark terror, I'd have run screaming in the opposite direction. But I didn't know. And I would not know until after I had plunged headlong into hell.

Class in Session

The day finally arrived, the day when supernatural powers beyond anything I had ever observed in the fortune-teller would begin to be mine. I drove with mounting excitement to the Sheraton, where the introductory mind-control lecture would be held.

The instructor appeared to be in his middle twenties, intelligent-looking, neatly dressed. There was nothing outward to distinguish him or his 20-odd listeners from people at a typical organization meeting. He told us that after the one-week course, we would be able to, among other things, control our weight, improve our memories, know what other people were thinking, cure illnesses, and better our finances.

It sounded too good to be true. But it had to be legitimate. There was a money-back guarantee. Anyone who couldn't demonstrate real psychic ability by passing an acid test at the end of a week would have his money refunded.

As the instructor talked on, I knew I was going to make it big. All my former failures, those I had pretended were successes, faded. It was as if my life was beginning all over again. Right, this time. Goodbye frustration and failure, spinning my wheels, going nowhere. Hello happiness, going somewhere.

The first two days of class we learned how to relax. The object was to lower the speed of our brain waves to the state that occurs in sleep. After reaching this level, we were told to imagine that we had a counselor in our head. The counselor would be able to answer any questions we might ask, to perform any test we asked of him.

I listened intently to all the instructor told us, practiced relaxing to lower my brain waves, got acquainted with my counselor, and was ready for the acid test the last day of the course.

The instructor gave me the name of a woman I had never heard of. I closed my eyes, lowered my brain waves, and began to meditate. In a few moments, I saw a stick figure of a woman in my imagination. She had a large "X" over one of her breasts. "Could she have cancer of the breast?" I blurted.

"That's right, Sid! That's right!" The instructor applauded, and the class joined him. I had passed the test. Supernatural power was mine.

When I went to the office the next morning, I could hardly wait to experiment with my new talent. My boss passed by my office and I called him in, asking him to give me the name of someone I didn't know—someone who was sick. My boss looked at me as if he thought I had flipped my lid, but he gave me the name of a man.

I closed my eyes, lowered my brain waves, and suddenly, without warning, I felt my arms begin to shake. "Why, that's exactly what my father does!" My boss exclaimed, obviously as surprised as I was. "Could he have Parkinson's disease?" I heard myself saying. I didn't know what the disease was nor anything about its symptoms. The name just came to me.

"Yes, that's it!" My boss said, excitedly rising from his chair. Then I told him that I didn't need to shake my arms anymore. "That's right!" He exclaimed again. "Yesterday my father started taking a new medication, and his shaking was controlled!"

Wow! This new ability was terrific. The power seemed to be increasing all the time. Yesterday I only had visions; today I feel the symptoms. I wonder what new thing will happen tomorrow? The power was real all right. And the more I experimented, the more uses I found for it.

One afternoon I was lost in the maze of roads winding through a park, and I said, "Counselor, direct me home." I made turns without hesitation on streets that were totally unfamiliar to me and found myself home in record time.

If I needed a parking space, all I had to do was ask that a space be available.

It didn't matter how hard the situation was, my counselor was able to take care of it. There was no telling how high I would climb with all this supernatural power at my disposal.

Almost as quickly as I thought of something I wanted, without my saying a word people began doing my will. All I had to do was ask. I would never wait for anything again. I had found an illimitable pot of gold at the end of an unfading rainbow.

One of my first thoughts, when I realized I could have anything I wanted, was that I shouldn't work for anyone else ever again. I should go back into business for myself. This time, I was bound to prosper.

Almost as soon as I had the thought, Jim Fisk, an attorney whom I knew only casually, just happened to drop by my office. "Sid," he said, "I've been thinking that you just might want to go back into business for yourself. In case you do, I have some extra office space available in my building. We'd be glad to let you have it free until you get on your feet. We'll supply your phone and secretary. You might even be able to sell some stock in our company and make some extra commissions for yourself for a starter."

After he left, I thought I'd check with my new power to see what he thought about Fisk's offer. "Counselor, make me money," I said.

Immediately I was led to open the dictionary at random and point to a word. When I looked down, my finger was on the word "anchor." That was the name of a mutual fund company I had worked with one time in the past. I called them up, and the regional man said they would be delighted for me to open my own office and go into business representing them. Just like that. And just like that I resigned from my job and set up shop in my free office.

What Is the Source of Your Power?

At the time I set up my own office, I was ignorant of the fact that Jim Fisk, the president of the computer company that gave me the free space, was a Bible believer. That was bad enough, but even worse, Jim had all the "Jesus people" in town trooping through his offices, and they had prayer meetings morning, noon, and night.

Somehow, although I thought they were all kooks, I liked them. They were more than nice to me, projecting a kind of love and acceptance I had never experienced before. And they did it even though they didn't approve of my mind-control involvement. Well, I was glad they had that kind of love, but it wasn't for me.

Soon after I had moved into my new free office, I met Art Lane. He was tall, well-built, distinguished-looking with prematurely gray hair, and very articulate. Art had every quality a man of the world ought to have, and I came to admire him greatly. But there was something strange about him.

Although Art was a Jew, he attended the Bible studies with the Gentile guys in the office building. I couldn't understand why a Jew would be studying the Scriptures with a bunch of Gentiles. It didn't make sense, but it did arouse my curiosity, so I began attending the sessions, too.

I gave them a hard time, questioning everything they said and ridiculing their faith. But they didn't throw me out. They didn't even give me harsh answers. Gradually it dawned on me that they were praying for me! That made me laugh. It was utterly ridiculous. But if it suited them, let them go ahead. I was glad for my free office and the friendship that gave and gave and gave without requiring anything from me.

One day Art Lane stopped by my office to talk about the insurance business. We talked about other things, too. He told me that he himself had come to "know the Lord" through reading the Hebrew Scriptures and understanding that Yeshua—Hebrew for Jesus—was the One who had fulfilled all the prophecies about the coming Messiah. Then he asked me a question.

"Sid, do you have a Bible?"

"Well, no," I admitted.

"I'll bring you one the next time I drop by," he promised. "But in the meantime..."

Art opened his Bible and showed me some Scriptures telling about the Messiah who was to come and some additional Scriptures in the New Covenant that showed that a Jew named Yeshua had fulfilled every single Messianic prophecy.

I was bored with the whole business. "Look, Art," I interrupted, "if the Messiah had already come, the rabbi in our synagogue would surely have told us all about it..."

"Oh, but that's part of the prophecy, too, Sid," Art smiled. Then he pointed to some verses in the book of the prophet Isaiah, and I read: *"Who hath believed our report? and to whom is the arm of the Lord revealed?...He is despised and rejected of men...and we esteemed him not"* (Isa. 53:1,3 KJV).

"You see, Sid," Art went on, "if we Jews had received Yeshua when He came, He would not have been the Messiah." With that intriguing remark hanging in the air, Art left my office. But the gleam in his eye warned me that he was in league with the Bible believers who were praying for me.

Well, they could pray all they wanted. But I was quite satisfied with my own life, thank you. Being separated from my wife, I had freedom to come and go as I pleased, and with my fast-growing mind-control powers, I would soon have the material world on a string. If there was a Messiah, I didn't need Him for anything.

Another one of the men in the office building who attended the Bible study and prayer meetings was Gene Griffin. He was an inventor who had spent a year in a kibbutz, a community farm in Israel. I thought it strange that a Gentile would take a year out of his life just to help Israel. And I noticed something else strange about Gene. He didn't act like a businessman or an inventor. It seemed that every time I looked at him, he was reading the Bible.

"You know, Sid," Gene said to me one day, "your God, the God of Abraham, and Isaac, and Jacob, is not pleased with your involvement in mind control. He condemns all New Age, occult practices."

"What do you know about my God?" I challenged.

"Plenty," he assured me. "Because there's only one God. My God is the same as your God. And if you'll read the eighteenth chapter of Deuteronomy in your own Tanakh, your Jewish Bible, especially the ninth through the twelfth verses, God's opinion about the occult will be plain to you."

I picked up the Bible Art had given me a few days previously, thumbed to Deuteronomy and read:

When thou art come into the land which the Lord thy God giveth thee, thou shalt not learn to do after the abominations of those nations. There shall not be found among you any one that maketh his son or his daughter to pass through the fire, or that useth divination, or an observer of times, or an enchanter, or a witch. Or a charmer, or a consulter with familiar spirits, or a wizard, or a necromancer. For all that do these things are an abomination unto the Lord... (Deuteronomy 18:9-12 KJV).

Talk about relevance! The Scripture made it sound as if reading my horoscope (observer of times), visiting my fortune-teller (divination), and consulting my counselor or channeling (consulting with familiar spirits) were things not pleasing to God. They were actually abominations! But what was this "necromancer?" I looked it up in the dictionary. It meant to communicate with the dead.

So séances are wrong? What about reincarnation?

Gene said, "Those who claim to be reincarnated and those who communicate "from the dead" at séances are not our loved ones but are familiar spirits who know everything about our deceased loved ones. They even know the events of history because they existed during those events. These spirits are looking for a body to inhabit. That's how channeling really operates.

"Reincarnation and the laws of karma say you keep coming back until you are perfect. The Bible says *'...man is destined to die once, and after that to face judgment'"* (Heb. 9:27 NIV).

"Even if you could come back, it would not make you righteous. We only become righteous when we receive the free gift of the Messiah's righteousness. A true Christian or Messianic Jew will never be more righteous than at the moment he makes Yeshua Lord. We are *"... the righteousness of God in Him"* (2 Cor. 5:21). And you can't get any more righteous than that!"

"Aw, that can't mean what you think it does," I told Gene, closing the book. "Just like I've been telling you guys, God's in charge of all knowledge. Why, He probably wants us to explore every avenue of knowledge—supernatural, natural, the whole bit. Everything we can learn about good or evil is to our benefit."

"Ever hear what happened to Adam and Eve when they nibbled at the fruit of the tree of the knowledge of good and evil?" Gene asked.

"Fer cryin" out loud! How naive can you get?" I exploded. "Don't you guys realize that these things have been handed down and handed down from one generation to the next? There are many difficulties in translating any language, and probably so many errors have crept in the Scriptures that what they say now isn't even remotely related to what the original said."

I didn't realize I had been shouting until Gene answered me in a super-soft voice, telling me that God had protected the authenticity of the Bible in supernatural ways. But I wasn't buying any of that.

The Prayer that Changed Everything

The next afternoon, I was trying to talk Jim Fisk into digging into his subconscious mind through mind control. Apparently he had had more than enough of my hassling, because after a while he put his hands over his ears. When I took the hint and shut up, he let me have it.

"Look, Sid. I don't want to talk to you anymore about it. I don't want to argue with you. I can't handle it. Tell you what you can do. You won't take my word for anything; you won't take the Bible's word for anything. OK. But why don't you ask God who Jesus is?" With that, he strode out of the office.

I hadn't told Jim I would ask God about that, but it was an interesting question to think about. I wondered what God would tell me if I did ask Him. But God had never told me anything before. And I wasn't in the habit of asking Him anything.

"Look," I told myself, "I'll accept that this Jesus was a man, a real historic figure. And He probably was a good teacher, lived a moral and upright life…. But if that's all He was," I interrupted myself, "why are people so all-fired excited about Him two thousand years later, just as if He's still alive?"

That was another interesting question. But it hung in the air, unanswered and unanswerable.

At that moment, I happened to notice a little white leaflet parked on the corner of my desk. Jim Fisk had handed it to me one day. I had flipped through without reading it and had put it down on my desk where it had rested, undisturbed. For some reason, I picked up the leaflet now and began reading.

"Have you heard of the four spiritual laws?" The cover asked. I hadn't, so I read on.

The leaflet was simple, easy to read. The first law said that God loved me and that He had a plan for my life. Well, that was all right. I had a plan for my life, too; I wanted to be famous and rich. God's plan couldn't beat that.

The second law said that man is sinful and separated from God. And the punishment for sin was eternal separation from God at death with no chance of reversing it. Then the third law said that Jesus, Yeshua in Hebrew, was God's remedy for man's sin and separation from Him. Yeshua lived a perfect life and died as my substitute. The fourth law said that in order for a man to have this substitution, he had to "receive Jesus…by personal invitation."

After the four spiritual laws had been explained, there was a page with a prayer on it that a person could pray to invite this Jesus to live inside of him.

I wasn't really interested in doing that, but I figured it couldn't hurt anything. Sitting in my chair, I read the prayer aloud, very softly so that if anyone happened to come in they wouldn't know what I was up to:

Lord Jesus, forgive my sins. I'm sorry. I open the door of my life and receive You as my Savior and Lord. Live inside of me. Take control of the throne of my life. Make me the kind of person You want me to be. Thank You for coming into my life and for hearing my prayer as You promised.

That was all there was to it. When I had finished reading the prayer, I didn't feel any different. No lights flashed; I didn't hear anything. I figured the prayer hadn't "worked." Well, that was perfectly all right with me. I had just read it for kicks anyway. I had known all along that there wasn't anything to all this Jesus business, and now I was satisfied that I had proved it. But there was something supernatural about that prayer, and despite my not feeling anything, God now had access to my life.

Power

At quitting time that afternoon, Gene Griffin stuck his head in the door, breaking into my thoughts with a startling question. "Sid, if God says that all who dabble in the occult are an abomination to Him, guess where your supernatural power is coming from?"

Gene just stood there, waiting for my answer. But I didn't have one! Where was the power coming from?

Fear hit me for a split second. Was there a devil? Could I be in league with him? Could the devil be the source of my power in mind control? It couldn't be. That bit about the devil was just superstitious nonsense. I snapped back to my senses.

"Look, Gene. Like I told you, I don't believe the Bible we have today is the Bible God wrote originally. Man has changed it over the centuries. And there probably isn't such a thing as the devil."

Gene didn't answer. He just smiled and slipped quietly from my office, leaving me to argue with myself. Even though I didn't understand all of that Deuteronomy scripture and I wasn't sure the Bible was the Word of God, the thought that I might be in league with the devil was planted in my mind, and it began to grow.

I decided to get the answer from the mind-control people themselves. I would ask them where the power was coming from. They would know.

That night I went to see my local instructor. "Bill, just where does this power we use in mind control come from?"

"Search me, Sid," he said. "I don't know. I've never given it any thought, actually."

He didn't know! The man who had tapped me into my counselor didn't know where the power came from!

Bill saw the fear in my face. "Sid, maybe you'd better not take the advanced course," he suggested. "I'll refund your money. But if you really want an answer to your question, I'll arrange a meeting for you with the top instructor in mind control in the country." I jumped at the offer. The meeting was scheduled for two weeks from that day in Harrisburg, Pennsylvania.

I could hardly wait to tell Gene about it. "You and your friends and your Bible can go with me to Harrisburg," I said, planning it all out in my mind. "You can sit on one side of the table and the mind-control man on the other. I'll sit in the middle, and may the best power win."

But Gene said he'd have to pray about it first, and after he had prayed, he told me that God didn't want him to go to the meeting with me. I exploded. That messed up my beautiful plan, and when the day came, I found myself on the road to Harrisburg feeling more foolish with every passing mile. I felt as if I was taking the trip to defend the Bible, a book I didn't even believe in.

When I was seated across a luncheon table from the instructor, we talked about everything except the burning subject until the waitress brought our dessert. I began by asking, "What do you think of evil?"

He laughed at the foolishness of my question before he dismissed it with an unequivocal answer, "There's no such thing as evil." He was so cocksure I knew he had to be right. How humiliating it would be to argue with someone who spoke with such authority.

Almost apologetically I showed him the Bible and asked him what he thought about it. He smiled and said, "It's a good book, but there are lots of good books." His manner suggested that any fool would know that.

To my great relief, before I could ask him anything else, he called for his check and said he had to be going. His parting remark was, "By the way, Mr. Roth, the next time you want to ask me something, no need to drive all these miles to do it. Don't pick up your telephone either. Just address your thoughts to me, and I'll pick them up and send your answers back, mind to mind. Cheaper than postage, you know, and a whole lot faster service." He slid a tip under the edge of his plate and strode to the cash register and then out of the restaurant.

I just sat there with my mouth hanging open. Boy! Think of how tremendous his powers were. Just wait until mine were that developed! Mind control was really the thing. I would stop listening to my kooky religious friends who were trying to scare me out of using it.

They could stay back in the boondocks if they wanted. I would get ahead with my life.

Seed of Fear

At the next mind-control meeting I attended, someone told me that a friend of his had used his mind-control powers on a jockey at a horse race, causing him to fall from his horse and nearly get killed. The accident let the mind-control guy's nag win the race! Wow, that's power, I thought. But some long-dormant vestige of conscience in me bristled at the thought that mind-control power could be used to hurt somebody. I had been told it could only be used for good.

At the same meeting, some of the more advanced students were asking their counselors what they would be doing in the future. I asked the most advanced student what his counselor saw me doing a year from now.

"Just a minute, Sid, and I'll find out," he said. He closed his eyes, lowered his brain waves, and almost immediately his eyes flew open. There was a startled look on his face.

"Sid, I don't understand. My counselor has always been a perfect gentleman with me, but when I asked him what you would be doing a year from today, he started cursing and using all kinds of vulgarity. And he refused to answer my question."

The instructor had no explanation for this strange kind of behavior from a counselor. He'd never encountered such a thing before, he said. What was wrong? Did the counselor see something so horrible he couldn't mention it? The seed of fear in me began to sprout and push upward.

At another meeting a few days later, the whole class went into deep meditation. Something new happened! I saw myself come out of myself! I was so excited I came out of my meditation and breathlessly told the woman next to me about it. "Oh, Sid," she said, "I'm so happy for you! You have just found your astral soul. Now you can really have everything you want, greater power than you ever dreamed."

For a few moments, I sat there quietly exulting in the fact that nothing would be beyond my reach. But then I felt her hand on my arm. "But Sid, let me warn you about something. Never let your astral soul take you too far from your body. You might not be able to find your way back."

"Not be able to find my way back?" I could feel the gooseflesh rising on my arms. "But that would mean...that would mean...I'd be dead...if my body was in one place and my soul in another..." I stammered. She nodded gravely, closed her eyes, and went back into her meditative state.

The seed of fear that had sprouted was growing in me. I shoved it down, rubbed my arms to make the gooseflesh go away, and resolved to be careful not to go too far from my body. The sensible thing was to keep my body in full view at all times. That way, I could always find my way back. Satisfied that such a precaution would be sufficient to prevent anything bad from happening to me, I continued to exercise my powers.

At a mind-control meeting the next week, the subject of astral projection came up again. The instructor explained that every time we sleep, our astral soul goes for a walk. I nearly fell out of my chair. The pricklings of fright were chilling my flesh again. When I was awake, I could control my comings and goings, but how could I do so when I was asleep? I shook my head, trying to clear it of my gruesome imaginings. After all, I wasn't asleep. I was awake. I was in perfect control of myself.

The next morning at the office I had an urge to do my dictionary trick again, this time without asking a specific question in advance. I opened the book, wrote down the first word my finger pointed to, closed the book, opened it at random again, and continued the process until I had five words written on a piece of paper. I did a double take when I realized that they made a sentence: "Refrain from this sinful dictionary."

Where was that advice coming from? I crumpled the paper, flung it in the wastebasket, and pretended to return to the work on my desk. But the disquiet inside me wouldn't settle down, wouldn't be still. I was seething with some kind of spiritual distress, something I had never felt before.

When Gene walked into my office a few minutes later, I told him what had happened and how I was feeling. To my surprise he didn't try to comfort me, he just threw his hands into the air and began to laugh and praise God for His goodness. That didn't make me feel any better.

Next, Jim Fisk walked in to see what all the racket was about. When Gene told him, Jim looked long and hard at me and said, "Sid, you look like you have a bad case of spiritual neurosis." Then he winked at Gene and made a victory sign, saying, "Looks like Sid's about ready for his breakdown, huh?"

Jim was obviously needling me. What were they doing? Were they trying to crowd me into some kind of hysteria or something?

The office was getting unbearable for me. I had to get out, so I threw some papers in a briefcase and got out as fast as I could. Could it be that my Bible-believing friends were right? Was there really a devil? By my involvement in the New Age, had I cast my lot with him?

Out of the Pit

As I backed my car out of the parking area, I kept getting flashes of incidents in my past, all ugly ones. My childhood tantrum on the train, racing around the table to get away from my father, copping out on my paper route, tattling, lying, cheating in school, refusing to staple letters together, leaving snarls of improperly done work behind me in more job changes than I could count, always trying to get something for nothing, profiting at the other fellow's expense, being unfaithful to Joy and thinking I was so smart to get by with it....

That was the afternoon of increasing terror. That was the night I went to bed with the mezuzah around my neck, the Bible under my pillow, fear enveloping me, and a broken heart inside me. That was the night I prayed, "Jesus, help!" That was the night I asked Joy to entreat her God on my behalf.

.Vhen I was a child I tried to imagine what death would be like. Since we never discussed death in our family, I concluded that life must end in nothingness. But that concept was so objectionable I did the only sensible thing: I stopped thinking about it.

Until now. For the first time in my life, the nothingness of death looked better than continuing a tortured existence. And with that thought I fell asleep from sheer exhaustion.

The next thing I knew, it was morning. There was a tangible presence in my room. The atmosphere was pure love. I was flooded with so much peace, I couldn't worry even if I wanted to! Sunshine streamed through my window and woke me up. I was alive, really alive. The fear was gone, the counselor gone, and in its place was an indescribable joy.

I knew that Jesus was responsible. There was a greater power in His Name than in all the forces of darkness that were trying to destroy me! I knew this deep within my being.

It was just as God had promised:

"I will give you a new heart and put a new spirit in you; I will remove from you your heart of stone and give you a heart of flesh. And I will put My Spirit in you and move you to follow My decrees and be careful to keep My laws" (Ezekiel 36:26-27 NIV).

I was free at last. And I was grateful, very grateful. Moreover, I knew that I had received the gift of everlasting life. This revelation, by itself, brought a major transformation in my thinking.

When I was in the New Age, I met people who introduced me to the doctrine of reincarnation. This appeared very Jewish to me because Kabbalah, Jewish mysticism, teaches that we keep coming back after we die. Later I found out that this is not Jewish but Hindu. Hinduism has hijacked Jewish mysticism.

True Judaism believes you live once and then you are judged by God. Daniel, the Jewish prophet, taught that after you die, there is a resurrection. If your name is not written in the Book of Life, you go to **everlasting** shame and contempt. If your name is written in the Book of Life, you go to **everlasting** life (see Dan. 12:1-2). So you really only have one chance at life. We need to live it to the fullest. We can only do that by entering a relationship with Yeshua as our Messiah and Savior.

Once I did, I knew my sins were gone. In fact, it was as if I had never sinned. You can't get any cleaner than that. Only when you are cleansed by God can you truly become His friend. A huge gap between heaven and earth just disappeared. It was no longer "God up there" and me "down here"—heaven and earth connected in my life and I felt God accept me as a friend.

Shortly after this experience, I heard God's wonderful, audible voice for the first time. He said, "Return to your wife and daughter." My marriage was healed. My heart was healed. It was like I was raised from death to life. Now my life is finally where it needed to be all along: right in the hands of the everlasting God. And the best is yet to come!

Commentary by Mike Shreve

A pivotal point for Sid was when he realized that the spiritual practices in which he was indulging were clearly forbidden in Scripture. But why would God decry fortune-telling, channeling, astrology, wizardry, witchcraft, spiritualism and other occult practices? Is He selfishly trying to rob people of legitimate spiritual experiences? No, quite the contrary—He is lovingly trying to protect people from spiritual deception and demonic influence.

God wants truth in our lives, not a false or counterfeit spirituality that detours us from our purpose and hinders us from a real relationship with Him. Many humble, sincere, God-loving people have gotten totally off track spiritually by subjectively deciding what feels right for them as they seek "spirituality," instead of following the instructions God has given in His Word. Sid would have avoided a lot of pain and wasted years if he had only consulted the Bible sooner.

Every seeker of truth should seriously consider measuring the acceptableness of their spiritual practices the same way. Years ago I visited the studio of a yoga teacher in the Los Angeles area. Janice was very involved with the teachings of Yogananda and the Self-Realization Fellowship. For 17 years, she had been deeply devoted to the practice of yoga and meditation. I sent her a copy of my book, *In Search of the True Light,* and she came to a meeting we conducted in the area. I found Janice to be a deeply sincere, peaceful, pure-hearted person. However, when I walked into the large room where she taught her yoga classes, the first thing that drew my attention were the pictures of various gurus sharing wall space with a large picture of Jesus (Yeshua)—as if all these persons were all on the same level.

With as much gentleness as possible, I pointed out that she was breaking the first and second commandments just by adorning her walls with those pictures and having images in her home (like statues of Buddha or various Hindu deities). At first she expressed surprise. Her questioning eyes were saying, "How could that be? I love God with all my heart!"

To support my assertion, I described the amazing visitation of God that took place when the commandments were given. After the children of Israel were delivered from the bondage of Egypt, they spent 50 days in the wilderness and then arrived at the base of Mount Sinai. God told them in advance He would visit them in a supernatural way on the third day—and it happened with intensity! The ground shook with the force of an earthquake, and holy, supernatural fire consumed the mountain. Black, billowing smoke poured up into the sky and blocked out the light of the sun. Then the Eternal One, the God of Abraham, Isaac and Jacob, spoke out of the fire to His people. Like lightning and thunder,

His awesome and powerful voice rolled across the desert expanses with absolute authority as He delivered His "Ten Commandments."

The first two commandments dealt with a critically important issue: the interpretation of the nature of God. The God of Israel said in no uncertain terms:

> *"I am the LORD your God, who brought you out of the land of Egypt, out of the house of bondage.* **You shall have no other gods before Me. You shall not make for yourself a carved image—** *any likeness of anything that is in heaven above, or that is in the earth beneath, or that is in the water under the earth; You shall not bow down to them nor serve them. For I, the LORD your God, am a jealous God, visiting the iniquity of the fathers upon the children to the third and fourth generations of those who hate Me. But showing mercy to thousands, to those who love Me and keep My commandments"* (Exodus 20:2-6).

I explained to Janice that this was no "Impersonal Life Force" that descended on Mount Sinai (a mere "cosmic power" could not communicate in such a way). This was the personal God of Heaven—the one and only true God to whom we are all accountable. The same God who outlawed channeling and witchcraft prohibited the use of any images of gods or the worship of any god other than Himself (practices which abound in Eastern religions and New Age circles).

Then I further explained, "Your guru, Yogananda, was born of a man and a woman. He was a natural, normal human being who lived and died and his body is still in the grave. He was not God. On the other hand, Jesus was born of a virgin. He was God incarnate in human flesh. He lived a perfect life, died, but then rose from the dead, and ascended to heaven. He now reigns as King over all creation. You have them side by side, as if they are on the same level. To grant equal respect to the picture of Yogananda is idolatrous. One is a mere man, while the other is the Almighty God."

Then I proceeded to tell her that if there were any statues of deities in her home, she needed to get rid of them—because they were misrepresentations of the true nature and name of God. They were myths, created by human imagination.

For instance, Ganesha is a very popular god in the Hindu pantheon, depicted as having the body of a human, but the head of an elephant. You see statues and pictures of this "god" in many places. He is supposedly the deity gifted at helping people overcome obstacles. Why? Because he overcame an awful obstacle: decapitation. Because of a misunderstanding, Shiva (another Hindu god) cut his head off. Then, realizing it was an error, Shiva tried to repair his mistake. So he sent servants to the earth with the instructions to cut off the head of the first living creature they found and bring it back to the celestial realm to place on Ganesha's body. Unfortunately, they found an elephant—so now you know why he looks like he is half-human and half-animal. This is quite evidently a myth, created by some religious storyteller. To pray to such an imaginary god who DOES NOT EXIST is an affront to the TRUE GOD, in whom we *live and move and have our being* (Acts 17:28). After realizing the words I spoke were true, Janice complied.

It took great humility on Sid's part to accept the biblical standard that challenged his spiritual practices. It took great humility on Janice's part to accept the revelation from Mount Sinai that challenged her spiritual practices. And it may take real humility on your part to set aside some things you have believed in up to this point, in order to experience the awesome love of your Heavenly Father. He desires you to know Him, but you need to set aside that which is false to find that which is true and enduring. That's really not too great a price to pay.

Endnotes

1. McCandlish Phillips, The Bible, the Supernatural, and the Jews (Cleveland, OH: World Company, 1970), 5.

2. Ibid., 6.

3. "The Mezuzah is a small case in which a small hand-written scroll of parchment (called a klaf) is placed. The scroll contains the words of the "Shema" (Deut. 6:4-9) passage, in which God commands Jews to keep His words constantly in their minds and in their hearts. The scroll also contains another passage (Deut. 11:13). The passages are written in Hebrew, and contain 22 lines of 713 painstakingly written letters." Judaica Guide, "Mezuzah," Jewish Information, The Mezuzah, http://www.judaica-guide.com/mezuzah/ (accessed April 29, 2009).

About the Writer

Sid Roth, co-author of this book, has investigated the supernatural for more than 30 years. His television program *It's Supernatural!* documents miracles and is viewed internationally. *It's Supernatural!* deals with subjects that most shy away from.

Email: info@SidRoth.org

Website: www.SidRoth.org

Chapter 5

The God Who Liked My Jokes

By Laurette Willis

*A teacher of Hatha Yoga finds the answers in
life after God asks her a "dangerous question"!*

When I was a little girl growing up in the suburbs of Long
Island, I felt very close to God—but it wasn't the God I
experienced in the church we attended. That God seemed
rather distant and stuffy.

My mother enjoyed telling the story of what happened the first
time we went to that church when I was three years old. As we sat in the
crowded sanctuary that hot and humid Sunday morning I screamed,
"Get me out of here!"

In time, I became accustomed to their reserved, traditional type
of worship. I memorized the prayers and knew exactly when we were
supposed to kneel, cross ourselves and answer in unison. I could
mimic Reverend Palmer's British accent when he said that Jesus is "our
only mediator and advocate." I didn't know what it meant, but I liked

the way he said it. I did my best to imitate his round vowels under my breath, until my mother would tell me to stop.

How different that was from my experiences with God in my room! I had an illustrated children's Bible and enjoyed telling my stuffed animals the stories by looking at the pictures before I could read the words. I would place them in a semi-circle around me, show them the pictures, and act out the stories using a variety of different accents and animal sounds. I enjoyed seeing how many voices and characters I could create. This ability with dialects came in handy in later years as an actor, storyteller and comedienne Off-Broadway known as "The Woman of 101 Voices."

I did my best to come up with a punch line at the end of each Bible story to make God laugh. I figured He had such a hard job that He needed a good chuckle now and then.

During the account of Daniel in the lions' den—when God spared the prophet's life by sending an angel to close the lions' mouths—I suggested the head lion mumbled, "No lunch today, boys!" Then I told my captive audience how God said to Noah, "Build Me an ark!" And Noah said, "Okay, God. That's right up my alley!" As an aside, I added, "Won't God get a kick out of that?" And I believed He absolutely did!

Hearing God's Voice in the Closet

As a small child, whenever someone hurt my feelings I ran home crying and hid in my bedroom closet. If Robbie Wolfe said I was fat, or Willie Woods pushed me in my little red bathing suit into the bramble bushes, or Karen Duzy didn't want to play with me, it was hard to hold back the tears. I'd run home as fast as I could. The moment the closet door was shut, I was safe. Sitting on a pile of shoes and toys, hidden among the shirts and dresses, no one could hurt me.

For three years, God met me in that closet. Tears streaming down my face, I shut the door and sat in the comforting darkness. At times

I would see a flash of light. Then a bright scene appeared on the inside of the closet door as if it were a movie screen. In this open-eyed vision I stood behind a curtain and watched an adult version of myself onstage in front of a vast outdoor audience. The grown-up Laurette had one hand lifted high above her head and appeared to be speaking or singing into a microphone in the other hand. In front of me were thousands of people who also had their hands lifted toward the sky.

I instinctively knew the people were worshiping God, even though I'd never witnessed such behavior at our church. The only time I'd seen people's hands go above waist-level was to hold a hymnal. Years later I learned that was a common way to worship God in ancient Israel and the early Christian church, and it is still practiced today.

After a few seconds, the vision would fade and I would hear a comforting voice over my right shoulder. "Everything is going to be all right." In my heart, I knew this was God's voice. His voice hugged me and gave me peace. "Everything's gonna be all right," I repeated after Him, sniffling and wiping my tears on my sleeve. Standing up, I opened the door and stepped out of the closet to face the world again.

This happened many times over a three-year period between the ages of three and six. Nothing seemed unusual about these encounters, probably because I had nothing with which to compare them. Whenever I was upset, I knew I could run into my closet and hide from the world, but not from God. He met me there and comforted me. He always understood, showed me what I believed was a vision of my future, and gave me blessed assurance. I could trust Him. He would never hurt or disappoint me.

The Wall Came Up

When I was six years old, something changed. I no longer felt that closeness with the Lord. It seemed like there was a thick wall around me, separating me, shielding me from everyone and everything. I felt safe inside this walled "fortress," but I also felt empty and alone—except when Mommy and I would play.

We'd giggle like girlfriends as we took long walks through the neighborhood holding hands. Acting out all the characters to the *Peter Pan* album I got for Christmas, we'd fly around the playroom singing "I won't grow up!" Snuggling together on the couch, we read *Little Women* aloud with English accents.

My beautiful mother Jacqueline was a petite, blue-eyed strawberry-blonde. She was brilliant and funny, with a voice like warm honey: an Irish colleen who spoke fluent Spanish and enjoyed parsing words back to their Latin origins. A frustrated actor and singer, she was an attorney and the first woman assistant district attorney on Long Island. I was so proud of her.

Although I could never believe it, I loved when people said, "You're just like your mother." She was stunning. I felt ugly. Sadly, this remarkable woman with the movie star good looks, brilliant mind, and tender heart became an alcoholic who had three nervous breakdowns and attempted suicide when I was a child. Things looked so perfect on the outside of our beautiful home on Long Island, but behind closed doors were pain, torment, and tears.

To compensate, I soon developed an unhealthy attachment to food. I remember running into my parents' bedroom and kneeling beside the bed. On a bright, beautiful mid-afternoon in suburban Long Island, Mommy was asleep in her darkened room. Was she depressed, or had she been drinking?

I was small, a little pudgy, with dimpled hands and knees, my round Campbell's-kid face framed with a brunette pixie cut. Tears pooled in bright amber eyes and flowed down chubby little cheeks as I patted Mommy's face. "Mommy! Mommy!" I cried. "I can't stop eating."

For the past hour, the little girl her mother called "Little Laurie So-Sweet" had been eating bread and butter, Easy-Bake Oven cake mix, cereal, and anything else I could find to comfort me while Mommy slept. I was six years old, and food was my friend.

It's surprising that I didn't become heavier than I did. I attribute this to my mother becoming the town's first "health-food nut," as people interested in nutrition were called in the 1960s. When Mom was following a healthy diet, taking vitamins, and exercising daily, she didn't drink alcohol as much—sometimes not at all, which was marvelous to me.

While other children's lunchboxes had Twinkies and Yodels with their bologna sandwiches on white bread, I had celery sticks and apple slices with my tuna sandwich on whole grain bread. I didn't seem to mind the kids' taunts about the weird food. I made it a game. I could eat carrot sticks like a rabbit and do an impression of Bugs Bunny to make them laugh. Ah—an audience! I loved it.

Over the next 20-plus years, food became my primary escape. If I ate enough, it numbed me. Then progressively, from the age of 13 onward, alcohol, cigarettes, drugs, reckless relationships, and spiritual practices were some of the things I used to fill the missing piece inside since "the wall" went up—the barrier separating me from God.

Numbness, I discovered, is a poor substitute for peace.

The Little Yogi

When I was seven years old, my mother became involved in yoga. A nice-looking Asian couple had a popular daytime yoga program on television. It was scheduled right after Jack LaLanne's exercise show. It seemed so harmless, so relaxing, and so *spiritual*.

The exercises relaxed Mom. Being an only child, my mother and I did almost everything together. We did yoga exercises together, too.

When she began teaching free yoga classes to high school and college students in our home, I was the little demonstration model. I loved the attention. My father thought it was all rather kooky, but he was busy building his law practice and didn't pay much attention to what we did when he wasn't home.

For several years, Mom and I visited Ananda Ashram, a yoga retreat in upstate New York associated with Swami Satchidananda. When I was ten years old, the Swami visited the ashram while we were there and "blessed" me. His smell was overpoweringly sweet. His long, wavy black hair was heavy with oil, and always looked wet as it flowed over his saffron shoulders. Perhaps I was supposed to feel "special" and "empowered" by the attention. I just felt uncomfortable.

During meditation times, I wouldn't keep my eyes closed. I kept peeking at all the serene-looking adults in the room as we sat cross-legged in the lotus posture, incense filling the air. I liked doing the exercises better.

For 22 years I was an avid student of Hatha Yoga, and was an instructor for part of that time. I also practiced Kundalini Yoga. During my late teens and twenties, I studied a variety of spiritual practices, seeking to recover the God of my childhood (though I didn't recognize that motive at the time). I just knew something was missing. Everything I studied, every conference I attended, every book I read, and every course I took was an attempt to find the God who loved me and laughed at my jokes.

My studies included a variety of metaphysical philosophies and practices from A to Z: Astrology to Zoroastrianism, Kabbalah, Mystical Christianity, Hinduism, various types of yoga, shamanism, Tibetan Buddhism, Universal Mind, Hawaiian Huna, Urantia, A Course in Miracles, and writings from other channeled entities, spirit guides, and Ascended Masters. Most of the worldviews I studied encouraged followers to "create their own reality" and "be their own god." Each held such promise, but left me feeling lonely and groping for answers. The people I associated with during this time were as lost as I was. None of the teachers seemed to walk in the love and joy they espoused. After decades of searching, I still could not find a person I considered to be truly "enlightened."

An Overwhelming Tragedy

In my twenties, I lived in New York City and was the typical struggling actor. I lived in the East Village and worked part-time as a secretary and waitress "to support my acting habit," as I put it. I fearfully went to auditions on my days off, but most of the time I drank white wine, watched television, and read New Age books.

In March 1982, I visited my mother, who was working as an attorney for the Thruway Authority in upstate New York. She and my stepfather, Fred, were separated, and Mom was very depressed. We got drunk together. "I feel dead inside," Mom said. I tried to encourage her with Tarot card readings and prompted her to get in touch with the light within, but nothing seemed to help. She said she felt as if she had no hope. There was a great sadness in her eyes. She looked totally lost.

A week later, I got a call from Fred. My mother had aimed a .357 Magnum at her heart and pulled the trigger. She missed the first time, but the second attempt hit its mark. The first bullet lodged itself in the bedroom wall, prompting police investigators to consider her death was a homicide, but they later ruled it a suicide. In a way, I was grateful for that. As horribly painful as her passing was, I couldn't stand the thought of someone else taking her life.

My boyfriend, Damien, and my stepfather tried to keep me out of the bedroom where Mom took her life. While they were out, I carefully wiped up her blood from the wooden floorboards and wall. I didn't want anyone else to do it. Crying, I held her hairbrush close to my face, closed my eyes and took a deep breath. Her scent was still there, but she was gone.

"You're Just Like Your Mother."

As the months passed, I drank more and went to fewer auditions. They scared me. Almost everything scared me or made me feel insecure. I walked along the streets with my eyes downcast. Talking to people frightened me, but it was easier after a few drinks.

Every so often, I would hear a voice in my head say the words that used to delight me, "You're just like your mother." Now the idea just tormented me.

A talent with character voices and dialects landed me a job with the First Amendment Comedy & Improvisation Company Off-Broadway. It was there that I was given the nickname "The Woman of 101 Voices." I did the one-woman performance "The Betty Boop Show" and appeared on television with the woman who did the original voices for Betty Boop and Popeye's Olive Oyl, Mae Questel. People said I was "the funniest woman they had ever seen."

While confident on-stage, I felt insecure off-stage. I continued my search for inner peace and spiritual enlightenment. I practiced meditation, chanting, aura balancing, chakra cleansing, psychism, channeling, and attempts at levitation and past life recall. I visited shamans, psychics, sweat lodges, caves, and shrines.

In addition to all these things, I studied bits and pieces from the Bible, but believed the Christian worldview was "kindergarten" compared to the higher truths I contemplated. I believed the answers were just around the corner in the next conference, the next book, the next spiritual high. I was certain I was just one experience away from being the person I longed to be—so I kept plodding along—like the proverbial donkey following a carrot dangling in front of its nose. I felt like that donkey, but didn't know what else to do. I was desperately seeking after the God of my childhood; I couldn't stop until I felt His nearness again.

Traveling the World Over

My mother had a little rhyme she would repeat from time-to-time when I was a child. As I sat on her lap, she'd hold me in her arms, gently rocking me and saying, "Travel the whole world over. Sail the deep, blue sea. When your wanderlust is over, you can always return to me."

I wanted to travel the whole world over. I felt that if I were to visit some of the sacred sites I'd read about, I would have a spiritual experience that would change me. I'd become the focused, confident, spiritually enlightened person I longed to be.

In the mid-1980s, my father became very ill with complications from heart disease and diabetes. I was grateful I could be with him in the hospital during the last weeks of his life. Even though Dad had not been to church in years, I learned that our pastor visited my father and prayed with him. That meant a lot to me, and I noticed that Dad was remarkably calmer the last week of his life. He didn't seem scared anymore or subject to fearsome apparitions. The man who could fly into a rage at the least provocation seemed peaceful for the first time in his life. It wasn't until years later that I realized what might have happened. Dad had made his peace with God.

After Dad's passing, my wish was fulfilled. I traveled to many of the world's sacred sites in Europe, the United States, and Peru. I spent thousands of dollars and countless hours looking for God and searching for enlightenment. At one spiritual conference, I was suddenly lifted 30 feet in the air looking down at the top of everyone's head—although physically my feet never left the floor. I felt giddy and elated for about 20 seconds, and then it was over. At an event in California, a famous channeled entity challenged me when I said I had a "tremendous desire to serve people." The supposed "Ascended Master" scolded, "Serve thyself, entity!" I felt hurt. This "enlightened being" had chastised me in front of 1,200 followers, and I felt like an idiot. How could I change the desire of my heart? "I'm hopeless," I thought.

I visited Stonehenge and Glastonbury in England, in search of mystical encounters. One morning, I rose before dawn and climbed Chalice Hill in Glastonbury, overlooking the site of mythical Avalon of Arthurian legend, supposed resting place of the Holy Grail. Standing alone beside St. Michael's Tower, I looked out over the fog-laden valley. I felt no closer to God—or Camelot. I just felt alone.

In Scotland during a meditation, I astral projected out of my body, flipped over, and was shocked to be nose-to-nose with my own tranquil self. Startled, I fell back into my physical form.

The more I traveled, the more desperate I became to have an encounter that not only gave me a spiritual thrill, but provided both peace and inner fulfillment. After six months visiting dozens of sacred sites in twenty countries I felt agitated and hopeless. God was not to be found in these places.

I'm reminded of what the angels said to Mary Magdalene and the other women who sought the body of Jesus at the tomb after His crucifixion. *"Why do you seek the living among the dead? He is not here, but is risen!"* (Luke 24:5-6). I discovered there are no sacred sites magnetized to hold God's presence. He's just not there. But the *"image of God"* who walked on the earth nearly 2,000 years ago is *"risen"* and now He's *"seated at the right hand of the throne of the Majesty in the heaven"* (2 Cor. 4:4, Heb. 8:1). His Holy Spirit will also indwell all who ask Jesus to reside on the throne of their hearts and be Lord of their lives. But these mysteries were hidden from me then.

Back home, I gave psychic readings and knew things about people I could not possibly have known through natural means. I later learned about what the Bible calls "familiar spirits," demonic forces that often remain in families for generations. An ability to hear or "channel" these spirits is a poor substitute for hearing and knowing the voice of God, as Jesus promises (*"My sheep hear My voice,"* John 10:27).

I sought God in the spectacular. I wanted proof that He was real. I later discovered, as the prophet Elijah did, that God is not often found in the intense spiritual fireworks our physical senses crave, but in the comfort of hearing and knowing His "still small voice" leading us through life (see 1 Kings 19:10-13). The supernatural experiences, while they thrilled me for the moment, left me empty, restless, and craving another "fix."

The "Dangerous Question"

After my parents died, I decided to leave a so-so career as an actor in New York City for the seeming serenity of a New Age community in the Ozark foothills. "Why stay in New York?" I asked myself. "Let me go where I'm happy and start my life over again." Since I didn't find God in my travels to sacred sites, I hoped settling in a community centered on a person channeling an "Ascended Master" would bring me closer to the source of enlightenment.

Not surprisingly, the change of scenery did not change *me*. As the saying goes, "Wherever you go, there *you* are." The empty feelings and unhappiness followed me from New York City. Although I would have insisted that I preferred being alone, in truth I was lonely. I wanted someone to love me for myself. In the end, it was the loneliness that brought me to my knees.

The first time I surrendered to God was the most difficult thing I'd ever done. Control has always been important to me. No one likes feeling helpless. When I became aware of my mother's psychological weaknesses as a child, I remember clenching my fists and saying to myself, "I will never be weak. I will always be strong." (Of course, it didn't work—I was a practicing alcoholic from the ages of 13 to 29.)

In the spring of 1987, I was driving home, when a "dangerous" question entered my mind. "What if everything you thought about God was completely wrong. Would you be willing to give it up to know the Truth?"

That question was dangerous because it led me to doubt what I thought I knew. I had a lot invested in the New Age and yoga—22 years of my life. I was even being groomed for a leadership position in my community.

That breathtaking question begged an answer. "If everything I thought about God was completely wrong," I said aloud. "Would I be willing to give it all up to know the truth?" Well, *if* I was wrong... "Yes," I answered, "Yes, I'm willing, if I can know the truth."

The next day I came to the end of myself.

April Fool?

April 1st, I was alone with my border collie Tula in my little house. I kept walking around the kitchen, calling out to God. From the depths of my being, I cried, "I surrender. I give up. You win. If You can do something with this life, You can have it."

In my heart, I spoke to the Jesus of my childhood. I asked Him to forgive me for making such a mess of my life. "If You want me to be alone, then give me peace," I said between sobs. "If You want me to be with someone, then send him soon, because I can't live like this anymore."

I fell on my knees and then on my face. As I did, it felt like a physical weight lifted off me and something I'd never experienced before—peace, like a dove, descended on me. It not only came *upon* me; it filled me. This peace was not the mind-numbing serenity I'd experienced in yoga meditation. It was not the blissful emptiness where nothing really mattered. I felt loved and embraced, accepted and fully, vibrantly alive.

His Peace: the Missing Piece

Peace. I'd never known how good it could feel. From the center of that peace came joy. This was not mere happiness or the giddy delight of opening presents. For the first time in my life I felt complete. Perhaps the best word for it is *shalom* in Hebrew—which means peace, wholeness, and completeness: nothing missing, nothing broken.

"For He Himself is our peace," the apostle Paul wrote of Jesus in the New Testament (Eph. 2:14). For me, His peace was the missing piece. I gave God everything I had, every mixed-up, messed-up part—and He gave me Himself: love, strength, and glorious, childlike joy.

The Jesus of my childhood, the One who laughed at my jokes, was not a religion, but a Person. You don't have *religion* with a person; you have a *relationship.* That's what I'd been looking for all my life—to actually *know* God. I wanted to hear His voice, to love Him—and to feel His love for me.

Oh, how I wished someone had told me sooner that I could have a real relationship with God! Why did no one tell me that all the knowledge in the world could not equal one spark of true revelation? By being willing to give up everything I thought I knew about God, I came to know the Truth—not a debatable philosophy or mindset, but a Person, the One who said, *"I am the way, the TRUTH and the life. No one comes to the Father except through Me"* (John 14:6).

That April Fool's Day I went from being a fool for the world to a fool for Christ. I don't worry about looking or sounding foolish for sharing the love of Jesus. How I wish others had been willing to be that foolish when I was so lost and alone—imprisoned behind the wall of separation from God!

Shortly after I surrendered to God, I realized I no longer had any desire to drink the bottles of Italian wine I'd consumed on an almost daily basis for 16 years. In God's great mercy, He removed the yoke.

Remember my prayer, "If You want me to be alone, then give me peace. If You want me to be with someone, then send him soon…" Four days after presenting that request to the true God, I met Paul. We were married three months later, on the 4th of July, 1987. I found out—God will give you the desires of your heart when your heart gets aligned with Him.

God Turns Stumbling Blocks into Stepping Stones

God has a sense of humor—and He never wastes a thing in our lives. He turns curses into blessings, darkness into light and stumbling blocks into stepping stones. The gifts and natural talents I enjoyed sharing from childhood onward, and the dreams I harbored for years, have found a far more powerful and fruitful fulfillment in my relationship with Him.

One of the reasons I left the theater was the emptiness: the applause no longer satisfied me. Since then, I've been blessed to present a number of original theater performances through our company, DoveTale Productions. Remember how the supposed "Ascended Master" rebuked me for my desire to serve others? Now that desire is being fulfilled in part through theatrical productions that have a real purpose. I've heard that the word *entertainment* comes from a Latin word that means "to serve." Entertaining others felt hollow in the beginning, because I didn't feel I had anything worthwhile to share. Now I do. I no longer entertain to be served by others' handclaps and accolades, but because I finally have something meaningful to give.

Since 1993, I've presented one-woman shows and ensemble productions in theaters, schools, and community centers through the Arts Council and Indian Education. I have long had a great love and appreciation for Cherokee culture and history, and now write, direct, and perform in "Under the Cherokee Moon" every summer at the Cherokee Heritage Center and National Museum in northeastern Oklahoma. These dramatic performances bring eighteenth- and nineteenth-century Cherokee history to life with actors speaking directly to the audience words attributed to the historical figures they are portraying. The audience becomes part of the show and interacts with the actors in ways that bring history "off the page."

I've also been amazed that my years in yoga have not been wasted, either. Since childhood, I knew that yoga was more than just exercise. It's a doorway to the New Age, Hinduism, and misleading supernatural experiences. Once I became a follower of Jesus Christ, I turned away from yoga the same way I turned away from channeling, tarot cards, and past life recall. None of these practices had a place in my life anymore. I liken fellowship with Jesus to drinking from a crystal-clear stream of living water. Why would I want to partake of anything less?

I was actually surprised when an idea for a Christian *alternative* to yoga came to me on February 25, 2001, at 10:35 a.m.—I remember it exactly! After months of prayer, research, and development, we started a fitness ministry based on the Bible, not on Hinduism. Over 125 postures are each linked to a different verse from the Bible, as well as numerous Scripture Sequences: multiple postures that coincide with longer passages like the 23rd Psalm or the Lord's Prayer.

We even have a series of postures based on the shapes and meanings of the letters in the Hebrew alphabet (*alef-bet*). I studied the Kabbalah in the New Age, but this teaching is different—everything points to Jesus as Messiah! For example, the Hebrew word for religion is "*dat*," which is a combination of the fourth letter of the alphabet *dalet* (which means "door") and the twenty-second letter *tav* (which originally looked like a cross, or the lower case letter "t"—and held the meaning of *sign* or *cross*). So, the ancient Hebrew word for religion is "door of the cross." How amazing is that?

And what a good way to finish my story. Thank God! I found "the door of the cross" and when I walked through it, all I was before became purified and useful to God's purposes in my life now. As I look back, I am grateful beyond words that I did not lose my life during one of the many alcoholic blackouts I suffered in my teens and twenties. I didn't lose my mind while dabbling in the supernatural, dallying in the psychic arena as if it were a sandbox, allowing my body to be used as a channel for strange spiritual forces, instead of a vessel yielded to God.

The God who laughed at my jokes and comforted me in the darkness of my closet has become the center of peace and light within my own heart. I would have never guessed that all the spiritual fulfillment I craved could be found in relationship with the JESUS of the Bible (YESHUA), the Living Word and Creator of the universe.

Commentary by Mike Shreve

When I read Laurette's story, especially how she traveled the world seeking mystical experiences at "holy sites," I was reminded of a well-known passage in the Bible—Jesus' conversation with "the woman at the well" (see John 4:1-29). After hearing of the Messiah's ability to grant to her "living water," this unnamed woman commented, "Our fathers worshiped on this mountain [Mount Gerizim—also called "the Mount of Blessing"], and you Jews say that in Jerusalem is the place where one ought to worship." The Son of God then responded, to her amazement:

> *"Woman, believe Me, the hour is coming when you will neither on this mountain, nor in Jerusalem, worship the Father. You worship what you do not know; we know what we worship, for salvation is of the Jews. But the hour is coming, and now is, when the true worshipers will worship the Father in spirit and truth; for the Father is seeking such to worship Him"* (John 4:21-23).

Two primary points need to be made concerning this discourse:

First, people tend to "hallow" or "enshrine" locations where significant spiritual events take place—far more than God does. He is not as interested in "where" something transpired, as compared to "what" was accomplished and "who" received from God in the process. For instance, I have been to that place hailed as the "upper room" in Jerusalem many times (where the Holy Spirit was first sent, like a rushing, mighty wind, to fill 120 disciples—Acts 2:1-7). The building housing that second-story room was actually built in the twelfth century, so it cannot be the original location, though it *might* be on the actual spot. Who knows? But even if it was the true site of that historic event, the physical location pales in significance to the actual outpouring that took place, nearly two thousand years ago, launching the New Covenant era. God's joy is not an edifice made with the hands of men. His yielded offspring are His true cathedrals of praise, the preferred showcase for the glory of His presence.

Second, Jesus indicated in this conversation that apparently, there are many "worshipers of God" but not all qualify as "true worshipers." As a teacher of Kundalini Yoga, my all-consuming passion was to worship my Creator. To the best of my ability, I did so around 14 hours a day. At my ashram, my students and I commenced every day at 3:30 a.m. First on the agenda was two hours of Mantra Yoga, then about an hour of Hatha Yoga, then about two hours of reading various "holy books" of different religions—yes, every spare hour was immersed in some kind of spiritual discipline.

I did nothing else: no entertainment, no television, no sports, no dating, no social gatherings—just "seeking God." With every breath, my heart was inclined upward. I distinctly remember breaking down, more than once, with tears streaming, crying out, "God, O God, am I ever going to know You?" I loved God intensely. He was my ALL IN ALL. I was a worshiper, some might say to an extraordinary degree, but unfortunately, I was not a "true worshiper." Why? Because certain vital criteria were not met.

Jesus taught that "true worshipers" worship the Father "in spirit and truth." But what does that mean? In order to worship God "in spirit," first, our spirits must be "regenerated" (spiritually made new) by the washing of the blood of Jesus and the entrance of the Holy Spirit into our hearts. This spiritual rebirth takes place when we truly acknowledge Jesus as Lord of our lives.

Worshiping God "in truth" involves five primary things—worshiping God:

(1) in honesty;

(2) in sincerity;

(3) with correct methods;

(4) by embracing the true revelation of His name and nature;

(5) and by applying the truths of the Bible to our day-to-day lives.

As a yoga instructor I passed the first two requirements with flying colors, but I stumbled over the last three. I daily used nonbiblical methods to try and reach God—methods even forbidden in Scripture, like the chanting of mantras. Also, I insisted on mixing the biblical revelation of the name and nature of God with ideas found in other religions, including false gods and goddesses created by human imagination (thus, breaking the first and second commandments—Exodus 20:2-4).

I worshiped and loved God intensely, but I never experienced true communion—until I approached Him using those methods endorsed in the Bible and until I embraced the true revelation of His name and nature. There are millions of worshipers all over the world generating heartfelt worship *toward* God who are deeply sincere. However, only those who abide by the Messiah's instructions receive actual union with Him.

This explanation may be challenging for you to receive, but you will never really know if it is true unless you try. Consider this analogy. I can describe an apple in detail to someone who has never eaten one (the color, the taste, even the molecular structure), but that person will never know what it's like to partake of this luscious fruit until they actually do so. In like manner, after the writers in this book have exhausted their ability to communicate the revelation they have received from God, the information is still insufficient.

There is only one way for you to *really* know, and that is to try it yourself. Pray and open your heart to JESUS today!

About the Writer

Laurette Willis is the founder/director of PraiseMoves, a popular, biblically based alternative to yoga. She has two PraiseMoves telecasts (one for children and one for adults) seen by a potential audience of over 250 million people globally, as well as certified PraiseMoves instructors on four continents. She lives in Tahlequah, Oklahoma, with her husband, Paul, who shares her vision of impacting the world with the Gospel of Jesus Christ.

Email: praisemoves@gmail.com

Website: www.praisemoves.com

Chapter 6

A Jewish Yogi Discovers the True Path

By Rafi Cohen

*An advanced yogi and follower of Sai Baba
receives a startling revelation!*

It was an ordinary day for me. I hurried home from sixth grade, got off the school bus, changed clothes, drank some milk, and ran out the door. I was in a rush to get across the street to meet with my friends. I grew up in Huntington, Long Island, in a typical Jewish home. Being a Cohen, my dad followed the rabbinic rules, even being kosher for a time. Yet, my childhood was far from normal. Across Woolsey Street in the woods there was a clearing where I had previously made a pit surrounded by logs on which to sit. I would go there and wait for my friends to arrive.

I had a lot of friends when I was younger. We would meet and talk. They knew me, I knew them. The only problem was that my friends... *didn't have flesh and blood bodies!* They were spirits. It had been a little over a year since they had first appeared to me as little bright lights that took on a "form" until I was finally able to recognize them as "persons." I could call them by name, talk with them and they with me. They stayed with me for many years. When I was a medium in New York City, they would tell me about other people's lives.

I remember often waking up in the morning and slipping out of my body through my throat. I would "fly" over the roof of the apartments and down to the parking lot where kids were playing.

After I saw what they were doing and how they were dressed, I would slip back into my body. Then I'd get out of bed, get dressed, and join them. Everything was always like I had seen it.

When I was 12 years old, I had a supernatural encounter that was to determine my destiny. It was about five o'clock on a beautiful, warm, June afternoon. As I walked out the front door of our apartment, I saw a man standing on a hill about 20 feet to my left, looking at me. He had long brown hair and intense eyes. He was wearing a long white robe with his hands outstretched. I remember seeing red holes in his hands. I instinctively knew this was Yeshua (Jesus). This was not a vision, but an actual appearance. Since I came from such a Jewish family, I didn't know much about Yeshua and anything I did know was negative. But two powerful things happened to me at that moment.

The first was that I felt an overwhelming desire to find that man in reality—not in a religion, tradition, or a building, but to find the *real* Yeshua. The second was an impartation, or an inner knowing of the reality of the realm of miracles. I knew that it was possible for all people who knew Yeshua to reach up into the spiritual and receive a miracle for their lives! That was the beginning of my 16-year search!

This is What You've Been Looking for

I graduated from Northport High School and went off to the University of Miami in Florida, where I majored in accounting. During my second and third year of college, I got involved with astrology, numerology, psychic phenomena, and a group called the Edgar Cayce Foundation. Edgar Cayce was a psychic, a medium, and a channeler in touch with spirit beings in heavenly places that would put him in a trance and speak through him.

My last year in college was the time many Cubans were settling in Florida. I met up with practitioners of the Cuban Santeria (a strange mixture of Catholicism, Yoruba African religion, Caribbean spirituality, and witchcraft) who taught me how to harness the spirits to achieve my "desires," how to move in control.

What is control or witchcraft? It is simply your will being done. When you desire your will to be done over God's will, or over someone else's will, you're moving in control. Then you summon up your "friends" in the spirit world, demonic spirits, to help you get the job done—witchcraft.

Shortly thereafter, I had another supernatural experience. I graduated from college with a degree in accounting, and went to work for an accounting firm in Miami. One day, as I was walking to work downtown, I suddenly saw rainbows around peoples' heads and upper bodies. These were called *auras*. In these auras I saw their dead grandparents, relatives, friends, where they worked, relationships, and even their names dangling like placards. I knew I had tapped into a deeper level of psychic, occult power.

I later moved to New York City and went to work for a "Big Eight" accounting firm on Madison Avenue, specializing in estate taxes and real estate auditing. Just a few weeks after I arrived, I met Agatha, an elderly Russian woman who was a famous psychic. I spent the next few years doing séances, meditations, channeling, and psychic paintings and healings. I also did the accounting for the New York City A.R.E., the Edgar Cayce Foundation, and did much astrology, numerology, Kabbalah, and psychic readings. Then after meeting with the Rudolph

Steiner Organization, I went to the Guertianam in Dornoch, Switzerland, for a summer program on anthroposophy, the study of psychic sciences.

But my life was soon to change again. After the summer program, I returned to work in New York City. One fall day as I was exiting the subway at 86th Street and Central Park West, my eyes were drawn to a man wearing Indian clothes sitting on a bench on the other side of the street. His long hair was in a knot on top of his head and his wide brown beard was resting on his open palms in his lap. A peace seemed to surround him as 40 or so strange-looking people sat on blankets and mats around him playing music, singing, and eating in the midst of the bustle and noise of New York City.

I walked over to them and stood in the back of the group to watch. Then Baba Gill, or "Freedom" as he was later called, looked up at me and began to speak in sign language (I learned he was silent and didn't speak with his voice). He said, "Welcome home, this is what you have been looking for!"

Satya Sai Baba

That was my introduction to yoga, Hinduism, Eastern theology, and a man named Satya Sai Baba, a world-famous guru who resides in southern India. *Satya* means "truth," *sai* means "mother" and *baba*, "father." So his name means the "mother/father of all truth." Sai Baba doesn't claim to be a reincarnation of Jesus, but the one who sent Jesus to earth. He claims to be God Himself! Millions of Hindu followers and thousands of Americans, Canadians, Europeans, and Asians worship him as God.

Sai Baba is known as the man of miracles. He waves his hand in the air and manifests piles of *vibuti*, or "holy" ash, that Hindus put on their foreheads for *puja*, or worship. Various sickly persons, even those dying of cancer, have received miraculous healings through his supernatural powers. I've eaten cashew nuts that just materialized in his hand. He fed 40,000 people during the Shivarathri Festival out of two buckets of food—rice in one, curry in the other. Cars empty of gas continued to run for hours. Photographs and jewels materialized out of thin air. I have since realized these miraculous manifestations were not from God, but from another power: a counterfeit of the true gifts of the Holy Spirit.

Under the Influence of *Shakti*

I was still in New York City, working full time in an accounting firm by day, doing meditation, yoga, and psychic readings by night. Then one night at three o'clock, something suddenly awakened me. There was a man with a red robe and black afro standing at the foot of my bed. I knew it was Sai Baba. This, too, wasn't a vision, but an actual appearance, which he was known to do. He pointed his finger at me and said, "It's time for you to come to India and be my disciple." Then he disappeared.

Obediently, I sold my piano for an airline ticket, my stereo for spending money, quit my accounting job, and removed my short-hair businessman's wig for the last time. I flew to Southern India and spent my first six months mainly around Sai Baba. I lived for his daily appearances (known as *darshan*) that he would make mornings and afternoons to the crowds of devotees. He would travel between his winter home in Puttaparthi and summer home in Whitefield, south of Bangalore.

Why do people go to such extremes to see and be around these who claim to be avatars (divine incarnations of high beings) or gurus (dispellers of darkness)? They believe that just being in their *darshan* (presence), or being touched by one, removes sin, and breaks the cycle of endless births, better known as reincarnation.

It was in India that I began to get filled with a supernatural power called *shakti*. I visited other high gurus with occult powers, became an ordained swami, and was given the name Swami Devatata, meaning "Gift of God." Freedom's devotees, known as "the family," would call me "Bless."

After six months, I went to Nepal. I walked 147 miles through the Himalayas, up to the Tibetan Border, with just a robe, a blanket, and a few utensils. Three months later, I went back to Patna, India, then to Delhi. Eventually, I flew back to Paris. In France, I came down with severe hepatitis and struggled up to Amsterdam for three weeks of recuperation.

By early fall, I was back in New York. After visiting my parents in Long Island, I went upstate to a yoga ashram (monastery) to "realize" God! I wanted to meet the "God within" and become one with Him, thereby knowing myself as "God." I spent a year and a half there, through the frigid winter in a tent-like teepee living with the Yea God Family, the enlarged group from 86th Street and Central Park West in New York City. A large percentage of us came from Jewish backgrounds, many were professionals and college graduates, and many were from dysfunctional families.

I had a number of dramatic experiences there, meditating for hours, going into *Samadhi* (yogic trances), and being completely overtaken by this force referred to as *shakti*. At the time, I thought this was just an internal spiritual energy or level of consciousness. I now realize it was a "dark spiritual entity" intent on taking over my life. Having yielded myself completely, it began making my choices for me—eventually pulling me south to Long Island, and New York City, and then to New England where I imparted this power to others. There I taught things I felt at the time were great spiritual truths, "profound" instructions like: "Be free, be happy." "Move away from pain." "Submit to everything. Don't resist anything." "God is everything and everywhere." "Love is the way to God."

I also taught: "The concepts of right and wrong, high or low, good or bad, Christ or the devil, don't really exist except as an illusion (*maya*) in our minds. We can transcend the duality of physical and spiritual through transcendental meditation until 'all is one.'"

They Kissed My Feet

People began gathering around me, and after a year we all started across the country in vans and cars. We later added a funky, old, furnished bus. Leaving Long Island, we first stopped in Hockessin, Delaware, then drove to Tennessee, San Antonio, Texas, Tucson, Arizona, and finally to Baja, Mexico. At each stop, I would sit on a bench in a park wearing my robes.

Seekers would come! And reporters came to write about the Family of Love that had come to bless their city. When we were hungry, people would bring us food or we would cook in the bus. Since we were strict vegetarians, we ate no meat, fish, or animal products. Being overweight was never a problem. When I left India I weighed 128 pounds. Some of the "high" spiritual experiences some of us had were most likely caused by severe malnutrition.

After leaving Mexico, we traveled through Southern California, stopping at San Diego, Los Angeles, San Juan Capistrano, Santa Cruz, San Francisco, and finally, Berkeley. We ended up at the University of California on the Berkeley campus. When I got off the bus, I walked into Sproul Plaza, the gathering area for students, protesters, dissenters and all the rest of the nonconformists, misfits and truth seekers, and sat down on a bench there for thirty-five days. People came from all over. They would kiss my feet, sometimes even falling over from the spiritual power.

You're Lying!

I remember distinctly on the morning of the thirty-first day, at about eleven o'clock, a young man with short blond hair, wearing a short-sleeved white shirt, walked through the crowd of people sitting on the plaza area in front of the bench and came up to me. He looked straight at me and asked, "Do you have Jesus in your heart?" Being mostly silent, I answered in sign language with a young lady interpreting for me, "For sure I have Jesus in my heart; and Ram is in my heart, and Krishna, and you're in my heart, too." (I had a big heart back then.)

Then the man asked, "Do you have the Holy Spirit?" I had so much energy in my body from meditating that when I held up my hand, three-foot rays of blue light came out of my fingertips. With this as proof, I answered, "For sure I have the Holy Spirit."

He then pointed his finger at me and said, "You're lying. Jesus is not in your heart, and you don't have the Holy Spirit. I can see it in your eyes." He turned around, walked away, and seemed to disappear into the crowd.

Test the Spirit Within You

Four days later, we drove our caravan across the country to upstate New York. We were going to a birthday party for Freedom, the man who had sat on the bench in New York City many years before. When we arrived at the "land" (so the yoga community was called), Freedom came out to meet us. He was talking again after many years of silence. He asked us to join him in Ten, the *satsang* hall, where he had an amazing story to tell us.

As I remember it, Gill (Freedom's real name), told us how he was possessed by a demonic spirit transferred to him from Sai Baba, that caused him to mutilate his body, hurt others, go into days of darkness and oppression, and then come out to manifest a spirit of the Hindu god, Shiva. He said two things happened that changed his thinking. First, he caught Satya Sai Baba, the "mother, father of all truth," in a lie. It was a major lie over a government visa. *"If God's name is Truth,"* thought Gill, *"How can he lie? Where can a lie be found in him?"*

The second incident occurred as a result of this yoga ashram having no electricity, no plumbing, no telephone, nothing connecting it to the outside world except a tank of L.P. gas used to heat water for a tub.

One day, a Baptist man from the city drove up to the "land" to change this tank of L.P. and left a tract on Gill's doorstep. Gill told us he was walking out of his yoga house with his eyes closed (being "led by the spirit"), when he tripped over the doorstep and landed with his nose on that tract. Gill took it as a sign from God to read it. He picked it up, brought it inside and read it. The tract quoted the Bible from 1 John 4:1-3:

Beloved, do not believe every spirit, but test the spirits, whether they are of God; because many false prophets have gone out into the world. By this you know the Spirit of God: every spirit that confesses that Jesus [the Messiah] has come in the flesh is of God, And every spirit that does not confess that Jesus [the Messiah] has come in the flesh is not of God. And this is the spirit of the Antichrist, which you have heard was coming, and is now already in the world.

Gill read it over and over. Within a few months his voice started to return and he received deliverance from the evil spirits by using the name of Jesus. He challenged me to test the spirits within me, as he had done. I retreated into a yurt (a small hut), sat on the floor, crossed my legs, and opened my mouth. As a Jew, I had never been in a church, but out of my mouth came, "*Shakti, do you confess Jesus as Lord? Shakti, do you confess Jesus as Lord?*"

I began to feel something like a ping pong ball going up and down my back, which I knew was this yoga "*kundalini*" spirit. Then it crossed my mind to ask Jesus into my heart. I was sure that He was already in there because everyone else was. But I said, "*Jesus, come into my heart. If You are the only true God, then I want only You.*" I then commanded, *"Shakti, do you confess Jesus as Lord? If not, I rebuke you in the name of Jesus."*

Within two hours, all of the *shakti* spirit and yogic energy left my body through my feet into the ground. When I stood up, I realized I was dramatically changed. I was the Rafi Cohen I had been many years before.

Thoughts began to come back into my mind. As a yogi, if I sat still for just a few minutes, my mind would be completely blank. Empty. No thoughts. Emotions also returned. Only hours before, I had had little feeling or emotion. I literally had been an empty shell through which a demonic spirit worked. As I walked out of that hut, I noticed all the auras, all the psychic powers, all the yogic powers were gone the moment the demonic spirit left.

I shared what had happened to me with others and found many had the same experience. Three days later, we felt we had to leave the community because of the many pictures of Hindu gods, incense burning, statues, and occult books.

We Need Help

We traveled to a park in Huntington, Long Island, where I had this "brilliant" idea: "Let's go to Virginia Beach to the Edgar Cayce Foundation, since he wrote lots of books on Christ consciousness, the seven spiritual churches in Revelation as Indian chakras (centers of spiritual energy), and more!" I did not yet realize Edgar Cayce was a medium in touch with the same kind of spirits that had influenced me (the Bible calls them "spirits of divination"—Acts 16:16).

We arrived in Virginia Beach on a Thursday morning, and I still cannot understand what happened next. The Edgar Cayce building is located right on the main highway on the oceanfront in Virginia Beach. We drove up and down the highway, but we could not find it.

Somehow, we ended up in the parking lot of *The 700 Club,* a Christian television network, located several miles away. I didn't know what this organization was, but some had heard of it, so we all wandered in. I was wearing my white robe, the women wore their Indian saris, and the men wore Indian pajamas. The people at *The 700 Club* talked with us, prayed with us, and sent us to an evening meeting at John Giminez's Rock Church. That afternoon, I broke years of vegetarianism on a fish sandwich at McDonald's. I was beginning to realize that it is impossible to "eat" your way into oneness with God. Besides, Jesus was not a vegetarian. If it didn't hinder Him, it certainly wouldn't hinder me!

It was a beautiful service that night. Over a thousand people were there worshiping the Lord, speaking in supernatural languages given by God, and praying for healing. At the altar call most of us went up for prayer. Pastor Giminez took one look at us and said we needed to be water baptized right away. That sounded fine to us, so the men went on one side, the women on the other and they instructed us about water baptism. They gave us blue robes to wear for the baptism. I felt right at home. I just took off my white robe and put on the blue one. I figured they just switched colors in Christianity.

The whole congregation stayed to see this. I was last in line, with about 24 ahead of me. One at a time they went under and came up singing and speaking in their heavenly, spiritual language (speaking in tongues) with hands raised toward heaven (see Acts 2:1-7; 10:44-48, 19:1-6). Finally, my turn came. The elders asked me if I wanted to be filled with the Spirit. I answered, "Yes." Then they lowered me into the water. When I emerged, something came from above through the top of my head and swept through my entire body. I knew it was the Holy Spirit. My hands went up and I immediately started singing in another language that I had never learned before. The water immersion experience was so powerful that I literally started to rise out of the water. The elders had to reach up and grab my shoulders to keep me down. Now, do you remember where the demonic spirit went? Into the ground. The Holy Spirit comes from above.

I walked onto the stage where the others were speaking in tongues, singing, and praying. I made my way to the piano and leaned against it, speaking in this new language. As I began to look around, I was surprised to see the Holy Spirit in the eyes of people all over the auditorium. I looked from right to left at the many people, then gazed back the other way and saw a couple from our bus group who wanted no part of this "Jesus stuff." (One Jewish lady left a week later and went back to India.) In their eyes I noticed another spirit—a dark spirit. Across the room there were a few others who didn't have the Holy Spirit in their eyes. I then remembered that man in Berkeley, California, who, three weeks previously, had pointed his finger at me and declared, *"You're lying. Jesus is not in your heart and you don't have the Holy Spirit. I can see it in your eyes."*

Since that night in July of 1976, my life in the Lord has been a walk into wholeness and healing from the damage done during my years in the occult starting at childhood. I didn't realize until years later how dysfunctional I was. I was running away, trying to escape the hurts of the past. I now know that it is *only* in God, the true God, that I can find acceptance, unconditional love, wholeness, and purpose in life.

The Real Thing

I am often asked how to tell the difference between a real healing or miracle from God and a counterfeit one. I have witnessed the following signs of a demonic healing:

1. The atmosphere surrounding the miracle is heavy, solemn, even fearful. Often, demonic healings occur in a dark setting, such as in a séance.

2. The glory for the healing goes to the person performing the miracle and not to God or Jesus. There is a "puffing up" of the

person, as if he were a god. This is so different from a believer in Messiah using the name of Yeshua (Jesus) and giving Him all the glory for the miracle!

3. There is an incredible bondage that comes over the ones involved in demonic miracles. They may be healed in the body, but become sick and bound up in their soul. I know of people afraid to leave India or the presence of a guru for fear that the sickness will come back.

4. Involvement with the occult in any fashion exposes the person to mental torment, constant depression, and sickness, mental illness, and poverty. If not broken, this torment can be passed on to future generations. I personally believe so many people are oppressed mentally, and are sick and anxious, because their parents or grandparents were involved in the occult (see Deut. 5:9).

In the Talmud, there are three miracles, known as "Messianic miracles," that only the Messiah and His true followers will be able to perform. In all my years in the occult and New Age, I never heard of these miracles being accomplished by a demonic counterfeit. The first is the healing of a leper. With all the lepers still living in the villages of India, to my knowledge, not even *one* has been healed by the gurus, shamans, or occultists.

The second is the healing of a person born blind, not just someone who later became blind through disease or an accident. That's why in the Gospels the Pharisees made such a fuss when Jesus healed the boy who was blind from birth. Recognizing this miracle meant admitting Jesus was the Messiah!

The third Messianic miracle is the casting out of a deaf and dumb spirit from a person and healing him. The Pharisees moved in deliverance, but they had to ask the demon its name. A deaf and dumb person couldn't speak to identify the spirit!

These three miracles were performed in Scripture by Messiah Jesus and are occurring today through His followers (see Luke 17:11-19, John 9, and Matt. 9:32-34). Through my ministry, in the name of Jesus, I have personally seen many healing miracles, including: tumors shrinking and disappearing, people with no eardrums instantly regaining their hearing, and healings from nerve and ear damage (Boyles disease), cancers, arthritis, joint disease, severed nerves in the back, feet, and legs, deteriorated vertebras and discs, crippling diseases, deformities, chronic warts, lupus, and mental illnesses.

From a stoic, wasted, searching state, God has restored everything. I am free to love, express my emotions, and fulfill my destiny.

What's Happening in My Life Now?

Since the time of meeting my Lord, I have come back to my Jewish roots and heritage, embracing the House of Israel. In this long journey I have completed the circle—now looking forward to the redemption of the land of Israel and the Messiah's second coming.

The question asked of me so many years ago still stands—"Do you have the Messiah of Israel in your life? Have you given yourself wholly to Him? Is He your guiding light?"

The Lord of Hosts, the God of Israel, is about to reveal Himself as never before. These are serious times because much is coming down. The old religious order is coming apart and it's time now to do the real thing!

How many years of people's lives have been wasted running after the things of the world and serving false gods that have no relevance: gods of wood and stone, gods of your mind and imagination, gods of myth! And on top of that, many have aligned themselves with spirits that oppose the true and only God—the God of Israel!

Let's turn fully to Him today and embrace all that He is doing!

Commentary by Mike Shreve

Rafi Cohen loved God intensely; he was seeking after God with all his heart. He devoted himself to intense self-discipline in his attempt to reach the highest level of consciousness. How could he get so sidetracked, even to the point of being "possessed" by an evil spirit masquerading as some "cosmic force" referred to as *shakti*?

There were two main reasons he went into spiritual error: first, because he did not understand the true nature of God; and second, because he did not follow the biblical instructions that reveal correct methods to use in seeking God.

Shakti is the Hindu word for the "sacred force" or "cosmic power" that moves through the entire universe. It is also the power that is unleashed within a person involved in meditation, that supposedly carries that person to higher levels of consciousness or enlightenment. It is said to have a feminine nature and to be coiled at the base of the spine (also referred to as the Kundalini or Serpent Power). Allegedly, when this "Kundalini Shakti" (the feminine personification of the universal force, represented as a goddess) rises up through the spine in meditation, it merges in the head or "Crown Chakra" with "Shiva" (the masculine personification of the universal force, represented as a god) and that person enters into "Cosmic Consciousness: oneness with God and the universe." Sounds spectacular, doesn't it? Such intriguing terminology drew me when I was searching for truth, until I realized the true experience of God is much different.

In the New Age and many Far Eastern religions, there is no differentiation between the "power of the universe" and "the power of God." They are one and the same. This "universal power" resides within every human being—and needs to be awakened. Therefore, God is reduced to a mere "Force." Strangely, this "Force" can manifest as both evil and good.

The modern-day movie *Star Wars* and its sequels have popularized this interpretation of the cosmic power of the universe—with Darth Vader, the chief villain, using "the Force" to manifest very dark, negative, occult powers and Luke Skywalker, the hero, using "the Force" to produce positive, noble powers and achieve righteous goals. However, the source is the same for both evil and good. That is definitely not the biblical view.

Scripturally, the power of the universe, the power of evil, and the power of God are three different things:

1. The power of the universe comes *from* God, but it is not God. Part of the power of the universe is an impersonal "life force" that allows living things in creation to exist and function. It is merely a part of the creation, not a manifestation of the Creator Himself.

2. The power of evil comes *from* satan and his demonic underlings. When Jesus appeared to Saul (later to be the apostle Paul) on the road to Damascus, he told Saul that he was being sent to the Gentiles to *"open their eyes, in order to turn them from darkness to light, and from the power of satan to God..."* (Acts 26:18). So the power that manifests as evil is to be distinguished from the power of God. Evil is sourced in satan, a literal, dark-natured entity who has willfully rebelled against God.

3. The power of God is His personal presence, and is outside of man until a true spiritual rebirth takes place.

One of the primary areas of deception for Rafi concerned the blending of all these forces into one. In his mind, everything streamed out of that one source—every spiritual force was, therefore, acceptable: the spirits he "harnessed" through Cuban Santeria to do his bidding, the spirits Edgar Cayce yielded to in giving his "readings," and the spirits transferred to Rafi from Sai Baba. But in actuality, none of these spirits were from God. They were from an alternate source intended to mislead him.

In unraveling this whole mystery, it helps to see that there are actually *two kinds of life*: first, there is LIFE FROM GOD, a gift that enables plants, animals, humans, angels and even demons to live and exist. Then there is the LIFE OF GOD. The first kind of life is impersonal; the second is personal. There are even two main words for "life" in the Greek, *psuche* and *zoe* (pronounced *psoo-khay'* and *zo-ay'*).

When Jesus urged His people, *"Do not worry about your life, what you shall eat or... what you shall put on,"* He was talking about physical life, temporal life (Matt. 6:25). The word used is *psuche*. But when Jesus promised, *"I have come that they may have life and that they may have it more abundantly"* and *"He who believes in Me has everlasting life"* (John 10:10; 6:47), the word changes. In these passages He is referring to Divine Life, the Personal Presence of God, the *"Spirit of life,"* which is *zoe* in the Greek (Rom. 8:2).

Generally speaking, *psuche* is the impersonal life-force of creation; *zoe* is the personal life-giving presence of the Creator. *Psuche* is natural life; *zoe* is spiritual life. *Psuche* is the human soul on its own; *zoe* is the fusion of God's reality into that soul.

Part of the reason all the yogis, swamis, seers, meditators and various occult figures interpret Ultimate Reality to be an "impersonal life" is because that's the only "life" they have ever known or experienced. The "personal" Life of God can only be experienced by entering into a relationship with the One who said, *"I am the way, the truth, and the life (zoe); no man comes to the Father except through Me"* (John 14:6).

He was the same One who breathed the "breath of life" (the breath of *zoe*) into Adam in the very beginning and filled him with the essence of God. But then Adam and Eve fell. They still retained natural breath, but the breath of divine life was gone. Praise God for the day when the resurrected Savior appeared in the upper room, "breathed" on His disciples and said, *"Receive the Holy Spirit"* (John 20:22). In other words, He restored the "divine life" (*zoe*) that Adam and Eve lost in the Garden of Eden. Now, thanks to Calvary, we can have it, too.

About the Writer

Rafi Cohen has traveled worldwide for many years teaching the Word of God and watching God confirm His Word with signs following. He and his wife, Dr. Carol Cohen, do intensive healing conferences entitled "Fuller Life" and "God Wants You Well." They also hold prophetic seminars and teachings on "The Lord of Hosts" and "Walking in the New Man." They have helped many people of different backgrounds as they minister God's healing and transforming power to the whole person—body, soul, and spirit. They have a big heart for Israel and relish their calling to serve before the God of Israel and His people.

Email: revrafi@aol.com

Websites: www.Godhealing.net

www.carolcohen.org

Chapter 7

The Highest Adventure!

By Mike Shreve

*A teacher of Kundalini Yoga at four
universities encounters the True Light!*

One of my favorite quotes comes from the well-known author, Huston Smith:

"Religion alive...calls the soul to the highest adventure it can undertake."[1]

I wholeheartedly agree with this riveting statement. The most exciting, most fulfilling, most intense adventure of my life has been the pursuit of Ultimate Truth and a real, personal relationship with God. A lot of different roads bore my footprints before the right path was discovered, but the Spirit of God did lead me—and for this I am eternally grateful.

It's easy now to look back and see the primary turning points: the songs, books, insights, experiences, relationships, and new ideas that triggered profound changes in my belief system and my behavior. Occasionally, I was simply caught up by some megatrend sweeping through society. Then there were supernatural influences: times when God Himself intervened in my life, and times when dark, malevolent beings made a play for my soul. Sometimes these turning points were negative and painful; at other times, they were positive and powerful.

However, they were all monumental moments. When I look back, I feel their significance all over again. It's as if pillar-like monuments have been erected in the depth of my being that I can revisit from time to time—until fresh, heartfelt worship ascends, like burning incense, toward the One who knew the end from the beginning and gave me grace in advance to complete the journey.

According to the Buddhist tradition, a young man named Siddhartha Gautama encountered this kind of "monumental moment" around the age of 29. Modern writers might call it a *paradigm shift* (a personal transformation that dramatically changed his worldview). Though sheltered all his life within the confines of a royal palace, Siddhartha dared to venture into the outside world. According to legend, it was during this excursion that he viewed the "Four Sights"—a sick man, an old man, a corpse, and an ascetic.

No longer could he remain spiritually asleep on a bed of princely ease. Having witnessed firsthand the suffering of this world, he was jarred from a self-serving mentality. The resulting desperation to find answers became, as author William Burroughs puts it, "the raw material of drastic change."[2]

The sheltered palace protégé made an unorthodox decision. Walking away from the opulent surroundings to which he'd grown accustomed, instead, he turned down the narrow and seldom-walked path of renunciation. Hoping to transcend the natural world, he subjected himself to intense ascetic disciplines. After many years of seeking, while meditating under the Bodhi Tree, he claimed an experience of Ultimate Reality he dubbed *nirvana*. As a result, to those who subscribe to his philosophy, he became the "Buddha" (the "awakened one").

My conclusions and Buddha's vary drastically in some areas, but I definitely relate to his passion for truth and the spiritual desire that drove him. A near-death experience in my freshman year of college proved to be the pivotal point for me. That almost-tragic night, I had the distinct impression that my soul was leaving my body and passing into a very ominous, pulsating darkness. I felt totally unprepared. I've heard it said that those who desire to die well must first learn to live well. I certainly had not been living well, so I wasn't ready to die well, either.

My near-fatal brush with this ever-present stalker of the human race actually helped me. A negative experience actually became a positive one, because I emerged with a new set of values. My former life no longer possessed an attractive aura. In my mind, the gyrating, sensory-pounding, party-going "music" of college life slowed down and decreased in volume, until it became a still picture: static, silent, and unattractive. As if suspended in time, I looked around and saw only empty and confused faces, even among those who claimed to be the most educated and informed.

I'd been a rock musician in my latter high school years, but the alcohol, the drugs, the absence of moral boundaries took its toll, and existence no longer looked very "*rock*-solid." Spiritual quicksand was slowly pulling me under and I knew it was just a matter of time before I succumbed. When I entered Florida State University, I strongly considered majoring in oceanography, but after my near-death encounter, a painful realization rose to the surface—"*Why spend my life searching out the depths of the ocean if I fail to search out the depths of my own eternal purpose?*" So it all appeared frustratingly unimportant.

An inward voice kept probing and prodding with admonitions similar to the one given to Horatio, in the Shakespearean play, *Hamlet*:

"There are more things in heaven and earth...than are dreamt of in your philosophy."[3]

In an effort to break out of the boundaries of "normalcy"—imposed by friends, by society, and by my own mind—I started exploring nearly every new philosophy or belief system that crossed my path. A longing for lasting answers drove me to become somewhat of a recluse. Once again, an inward sense of desperation became "the raw material of drastic change."

After years of being insensitive, I turned my gaze once again toward religion, more importantly, toward *spirituality*. I was raised a Roman Catholic. Until my early teens I was very devoted, but the idea that Christianity was the only way to God, to the exclusion of all other religions, just seemed too narrow-minded, too unreasonable. Besides, I decided I could no longer embrace something just because it was part of my cultural or family "belief system." I purposed to "wipe the slate clean" and start from a pure and unbiased beginning point.

Socrates said, "The unexamined life is not worth living." I resolved that beliefs left unexamined might not be worth much either. Intending to explore various religions of the world with an open mind, I embarked on a quest for "True Light." Even though I recognized I was studying the theories, opinions and supposed "revelations" of others, my primary goal was to experience God for myself. I had faith that something somewhere would prove to be my connecting link with Ultimate Reality.

Elizabeth Barrett Browning's words well describe my mindset at that time:

Earth's crammed with heaven;
And every common bush afire with God;
But only he who sees takes off his shoes,

The rest sit round it and pluck blackberries.[4]

Blackberries held no interest for me any longer. I was willing to "take off my shoes" and look at things differently. I was definitely searching for my "burning bush." All of this was definitely progress in the right direction. Little did I anticipate the unique turns my life would take before reaching my goal. The first main milestone in the road was...

An Encounter With Eastern Religions

I began reading a lot of literature that opened the door to new philosophies, metaphysical ideas and Far Eastern religions. Over a period of months I visited a wide spectrum of written works, like Ayn Rand and her philosophy of "Objectivism" (*Atlas Shrugged*), Herman Hess (*Siddhartha*), Levi Dowling (*The Aquarian Gospel*), Meher Baba (*God Speaks*), Helena Blavatsky (*The Secret Doctrine*), and books by various gurus and out-of-the-box thinkers. New phraseology filled up my mind, words like: reincarnation, karma, yoga, astral projection, soul travel, mantras, chakras, the third eye, nirvana, Ascended Masters, self-realization and "God consciousness." All of these concepts exploded in me with a fiery fervor to know more.

I joined an Edgar Cayce meditation group in Orlando, Florida. It was very easy to adapt to their approach because they used "The Lord's Prayer" as a basis for meditation. I had uttered this prayer thousands of times as a Catholic. Because it was already deeply rooted in my psyche, it became a perfect, nonintrusive means of introducing me to a new worldview. I was never disturbed by the subtle changes in the meanings assigned to various words or phrases. Yet the line-by-line interpretations of the prayer were no longer promoting a biblical perspective, but a metaphysical one. Not abruptly, but slowly and consistently, my worldview was changing. The tension Edgar Cayce felt between the new "prophetic" insights he received during hypnosis sessions, as opposed to his long held biblical beliefs, intrigued me. Why did he struggle for years in trying to reconcile the two views? Now I understand.

In the fall of 1969, I went to hear Yogi Bhajan, a guru from India who claimed he came to North America to help the "flower child," "peace" generation find their way spiritually. He taught us about *yoga* (a word meaning "yoked," implying that the devotee is yoked with God). The emphasis was not on obtaining a "relationship" with God, but rather, on attaining a "realization" of our inherent oneness with God (actually, an understanding that *we are God*). God was referred to as "the Great Computer" into which the right mechanical mantra must be "inserted" in order to bring forth the desired results. That clearly threw the responsibility on seekers to successfully "ascend" to higher realms of consciousness.

With his full beard, long black hair, and intense dark eyes, this teacher of Far Eastern mysticism was somewhat imposing and quite convincing. However, it was much more than the mystique surrounding this tall, turban-clad Sikh that attracted followers. It was more than the passion he seemed to display concerning his beliefs. It was more than just the stimulus of a new approach to spirituality. It was the promise that we could personally penetrate the supernatural realm and experience Ultimate Reality ourselves. This drew me and thousands of others to Yogi Bhajan's words and to the spiritual discipline he was propagating (Kundalini Yoga).

Attaining my "higher self" became the primary focus of my day-to-day existence. In between and after college classes, I used every available hour to pursue the goal of "reaching enlightenment." The Hindu Bhakti poet Surdas warned, *"Without devotion to God, you will make yourself into a stale crumb to be eaten by the tiger of Time."*

Appalled at the thought of becoming a stale crumb, the following spring, I decided to use my time more wisely, quitting school to "escape the jaws of the tiger."

Packing up my belongings, I left Florida State University in Tallahassee, Florida, to help start an ashram in Daytona Beach (a commune where yoga devotees live together to more effectively practice their disciplines). Every day involved hours of meditation and Mantra Yoga (the chanting of certain Hindu words and phrases designed to carry a person to higher levels of awareness). We also devoted ourselves to the study of Hatha Yoga. This centered on physical exercises (*asanas*) and breathing exercises (*pranayama*), both of which were aimed at opening the spiritual energy centers in the body (*chakras*).

Our daily routine included the study of various religious writings, like the Bhagavad-Gita and the Vedas (ancient Hindu Scriptures). Then, of course, there was participation in yoga classes several times a week. Every waking hour and every activity, even bathing and eating meals, was controlled by a prearranged discipline. We were motivated by the supreme goal of all ashram devotees—our souls (*atman*) blending into oneness with the Oversoul (*Brahman*). We were totally committed to the process.

Peculiar and pleasant things began happening to me: a deep sense of peace, occasional out-of-body excursions into the "astral realm," vivid spiritual dreams. The suffocating control of the natural realm seemed to be easing its grip. A kind of spiritual adrenaline surged through me daily—the prospect that I was wrenching myself free from what my teachers called *maya*, the illusion of this present world. I felt encouraged that transcendent love would prevail for me—that I, in an Adamlike sense, would one day awake out of spiritual sleep to find myself gazing into the face of my Maker. What could be better?

So I followed hard after God, until every waking moment was pulsating with the heartbeat of a sacred quest. Nothing can express the cry of my heart then better than the following quote from the "Sayings of Shri Ramakrishna":

If you fill an earthen vessel with water and set it apart upon a shelf, the water in it will dry up in a few days; but if you place the same vessel immersed in water, it will remain filled as long as it is kept there. Even so is the case of your love for the Lord God...if you keep your heart immersed always in the ocean of divine love, your heart is sure to remain ever full to overflowing with the water of the divine love."[5]

"Full to overflowing"... to be *full*: that spoke of satisfying my own spiritual need of intimate communion with God. But to *overflow*... that spoke of satisfying the thirst of others for spiritual truth. Though my initial desire in the ashram was to be *full* myself, day by day I began sensing even greater concern for the parched state of others. I needed to *overflow*. I concluded that a more unselfish focus on helping other seekers was the "high calling." I could no longer ignore the plight of a human race draped in spiritual ignorance. So I decided to branch out and start teaching classes myself.

Feeling strongly compelled, I moved to the thriving city of Tampa, Florida. Four universities in that area (University of South Florida, University of Tampa, Florida Presbyterian, and New College) opened their doors, allowing me to use their facilities for extracurricular classes. Several hundred students began attending. It was fulfilling. Changing other lives with my changed life—this was the continuation of a cycle, the evolution of true spirituality. A number of my students, desiring to devote themselves more completely, requested that I rent a suitable facility and start an ashram. Gladly, I complied.

One night during that time, I experienced a major, spiritual breakthrough: I was absorbed into "white light." I had the distinct impression that my soul exited my body and was drawn into a very intense and timeless radiance. Though now I have a different interpretation of what really happened during the phenomenon, I felt I was passing into the highest state of meditation. More assured than ever that I was truly on "my path," I intensified my efforts. I wanted to abide there continuously—to walk in a state of constant illumination.

Then something unexpected happened! A divine appointment interrupted what had become a predictable pattern of life. I wasn't even seeking for new direction, but God knew my heart. He knew my love for Him and my sincerity of purpose. So He intervened by orchestrating some very noteworthy events that brought about...

A Dramatic Change

Several key happenings took place within a few weeks that caused the most important turning point in my life. First, the *Tampa Tribune* newspaper published a half-page interview with me. The reporter questioned me concerning my beliefs as a teacher of Kundalini Yoga and reported what I was doing in the Tampa area. I was thankful for the exposure, certain this free publicity would increase the attendance in my classes.

Little did I know that it would also alert a local Christian prayer group to begin praying for me.

They cut the article out of the paper, pinned it to their prayer board, and assigned someone to fast and pray for me every day until my conversion took place. Several weeks later, I received a letter from a college friend who had also left school to study under a different guru. The content of Larry's letter was quite a surprise. It described an abrupt change that had just taken place in his life. Though he had been devoted to yoga and meditation, something had radically transformed his whole approach to the things of God. Larry excitedly shared how he'd walked into a church and heard an audible voice say, "Jesus is the ONLY WAY!" At the same time, the Holy Spirit fell on him and he was "*born again*" (John 3:3).

At first, I assumed this was just a synonymous "Christian" term for what the Hindus called *Samadhi* or fellow New Age seekers called "*Christ consciousness.*" But Larry insisted that this was different. The Far Eastern/New Age view I was promoting claimed a latent "spark of divinity" exists *within* all human beings that must be "awakened" to achieve "God consciousness." However, the biblical view explains that, because of our corrupted state, God is separate from us, and that spiritual rebirth comes only when we are washed clean from our sin in the blood of Jesus. Then the Spirit of God enters into our hearts from *without*. At that point, we are brought into true oneness with God. Larry's words were emphatic, "Mike, you'll never find ultimate peace through yoga and meditation. You have to go through the cross. You have to be spiritually reborn. Jesus is the way to eternal life."

I wrote my college friend back, explaining that I was happy he'd found "the path of Christianity" to be right for him. However, I also confided that some of Christianity's claims seemed illogical to me, and that it was far too exclusive—making it a "lesser path," an immature religious mindset. "All religions are different paths to the same God," I countered. Strangely, though, I could not get Larry's letter off my mind. His words kept echoing inside of me, even though their logic escaped me.

After several weeks, I decided I needed to deal with this issue. Dismissing Christianity without fully exploring its claims would be unfair—unfair to me and unfair to the One who claimed to be the Savior of the world. I realized I had never really given Jesus an opportunity to prove Himself. So I concluded, "If He really was who He claimed to be, and if I don't test His teachings, I might miss the very thing I've been searching for. Besides, if Jesus allowed Himself to be crucified for the salvation of the human race, I *owe* it to Him to at least open my heart to the possibility of His claims being true." So one morning, though it involved quite an inward struggle, instead of following my usual yoga routine, I decided to...

Dedicate One Day to the Lord Jesus!

I got up about 3:15 a.m. That was our normal time of rising in the ashram. Beginning at 3:30, we would spend about an hour doing various postures and breathing exercises. Then from 4:30 to 6:30 we would sit cross-legged and motionless, in what is called the "lotus position," doing various kinds of meditation. Usually we practiced Mantra Yoga. That pivotal morning, though, I decided to break away from the ordinary.

Purposefully, I went into a room by myself and sat down. Though it seemed spiritually incorrect, I prayerfully dedicated the entire day to this One Larry claimed was the only *"Mediator between God and men"* (1 Tim. 2:5). Several times I confessed, *"Lord Jesus, I commit this day to You. I believe, if You're real and if You're the Savior of the world, You will show me today."* Then I began reading the Bible, spending most of my time immersed in the Gospel of John and the book of the Revelation. I was especially stirred by the latter, with its powerful, prophetic visions, especially those verses foretelling that final conflict between the forces of good and evil at a battleground in Israel called Armageddon.

As I read, I kept praying. Even though I was fully expecting some kind of powerful, supernatural visitation (a vision, an audible voice) initially, it didn't happen that way. For about eight hours that day I continued seeking the Lord Jesus. Then, right when I was about to give up and dismiss the claims that He was the "Messiah," God intervened, and I arrived at my...

Moment of Destiny!

Kent Sullivan was a senior at the University of South Florida. He was an accomplished student, but his educational pursuits had not brought him the lasting answers or peace of mind he desired. A few months before, he had been following the teachings of Yogananda, a well-known Indian guru who authored a widely read book called, *The Autobiography of a Yogi*. Abruptly, though, Kent had switched from Kriya Yoga to Christianity.

Though I'd never met Kent personally, I was well aware of his unexpected "conversion." It was the "talk of the town" among those involved in yoga and meditation. Many of us were wondering, "How could he do it? He was recognized as one of the most advanced students of yoga in the Tampa area. How could he opt for the idea that Jesus is the only path to salvation?" "How could anyone who understands the concept of all religions being one ever depart from it?" Of course, as I pondered these things, I had no idea that....

Kent belonged to the very prayer group that was praying for me.

That divinely appointed day, Kent decided to wash his dirty clothes. He had a free hour in between classes. It was a perfect time to take care of a boring, yet necessary task. Carrying an armful of clothes, he got about halfway through the door of the laundromat when the Spirit of God spoke to his spirit saying, "Don't go in there. I have something else for you to do. Get back in your van and drive where I lead you." It seemed impractical and illogical. Besides, being a new Christian, Kent was not used to having his plans interrupted by the Holy Spirit. He submitted to God's design, though, thinking it quite peculiar. Of course, he had no idea that about two miles away...

The yoga teacher who had been the object of his prayers for several weeks was hitchhiking, trying to catch a ride to the University of South Florida.

Even though I had spent the majority of the day focusing on the claims of Christianity, I was on my way that afternoon to conduct one of my yoga classes. (Because I'd renounced ownership of all unnecessary material possessions, I usually had to walk or hitchhike everywhere.) While standing on the side of the road, I was still praying that if Jesus was "the Way," He would reveal Himself.

As Kent drove, the Spirit of God impressed him to make several definite turns, eventually leading him down a road behind Busch Gardens. He was still wondering why he was doing this when he noticed me, "thumbing" for a ride. With long, curly, brown hair, a long beard and loose-fitting Indian-style clothing, I definitely looked the part of a Western devotee to Far Eastern religions. Kent never picked up hitch-hikers, but felt curiously "led" to pull over. As I opened the door, my heart started racing in my chest, because...

Taped to the ceiling of Kent's van was a large picture of Jesus.

I knew this was no mere *coincidence*; it was a *God-incidence*: the answer to my prayers. My heart was charged with anticipation. After a few moments of silence, Kent blurted out, "Friend, can I ask you a question?" Without hesitation, I responded, "Yes!" He immediately asked, "Have you ever experienced Jesus coming into your heart?" I answered, "No, but when can I? I've been praying about the experience all day long."

Kent's face broke into a look of surprise. He didn't expect me to respond so quickly. He offered, "You can come to our prayer meeting tonight." I replied, "I don't want to wait for a prayer meeting; I've been praying all day. If this is a valid approach to God, I want to experience Jesus right now." Thrilled over my eagerness, Kent pulled out of the traffic into the first parking lot he could find. With the van idling, we sat on the floor in back. Carefully, he took me step-by-step through Scripture, explaining the true, biblical path to God. Then, right when I was on the verge of embracing the Christian approach, my own intellect became...

A Very Difficult Stumbling Block!

A compelling thought gripped my mind. If I was going to be sincere during this time of prayer, I had to first deal with some disturbing doctrinal issues. One by one, I brought up traditional biblical concepts that were very perplexing or unacceptable to me. With each question or comment Kent would calmly reassure me with the words, "Don't worry about that. JUST TRY JESUS!" As I pinpointed certain

Far Eastern or New Age beliefs I felt I could never give up (like rein-carnation), Kent kept emphasizing, "Don't concern yourself with those things, JUST TRY JESUS!"

Being a former student of yoga himself, Kent understood my apprehension. He could relate to the protectiveness I felt toward my belief system. He showed tremendous wisdom. He knew that if we got involved in some deep discussion over doctrine, I might turn my heart away from the experience of Jesus altogether. So he kept emphasizing the essential thing: that if I would confess Jesus as Lord of my life and invite Him into my heart, His indwelling presence would establish me in a position of sonship and oneness with the Father (see Eph. 3:17, Gal. 4:6).

Kent understood something I am very convinced of now. It takes a spiritual rebirth before anyone can truly comprehend the mysteries of God's kingdom. Because Jesus is "the truth," once He comes into a person's heart, He sets in motion a process of leading that person, by the Holy Spirit, into all truth (see John 14:6). So the most impor-tant thing is for seekers to first experience the reality of Jesus' personal presence. Then they can far more easily sort out all the related truths that surround this central theme of true Christianity.

Kent finally persuaded me. His logic was strong enough to nudge me into the unknown. Besides, I was so hungry to *know* God; tempo-rarily setting my intellect aside wasn't too much to ask. Just repeating a single petition seemed *far too simple*—but again, I was willing to try. We bowed our heads together and I prayed:

Lord Jesus, come into my heart. Wash me in Your blood. Forgive me of my sins. By faith, I receive Your gift of eternal life. Fill me with Your presence and Your love. I acknowledge that You died for the sins of the world and that You arose from the dead. I accept You now as Lord of my life."

I felt a warm sensation in the deepest part of my heart. It wasn't an overpowering supernatural sensation, but I knew something dramatic was transpiring, different than anything I'd ever experienced before. In my younger years, I served as an altar boy in various Catholic churches and attended parochial school. The nuns and priests inspired me with their humility, sincerity and commitment. But still, during that period of deep "religious" devotion—filled with traditions and ceremonies—I'd never received such a real encounter with God.

Paul, the apostle, called this experience *"the washing of regeneration and the renewing of the Holy Spirit"* (Titus 3:5). Though I still had many questions, the inner "knowing" that I had finally been restored to a right relationship with my Everlasting Father filled me up. I was confident that if I died, I would spend eternity in heaven. The peace of God settled like fresh dew on my soul. I was changed—and I knew it.

Vietnamese Buddhist, Thich Nhat Hanh, offers, "If we touch the Holy Spirit, we touch God, not as a concept, but as a living reality."[6] This was definitely my mindset as a yoga teacher, and I believe it even more intensely today. However, I now understand that experiencing something "supernatural" may or may not indicate an actual experience of God. I sincerely *thought* (as apparently Thich Nhat Hanh did) that I was experiencing the "living reality" of the Holy Spirit during my yogic disciplines, but after being born again, I realized that was not the case. There is no comparison between a mere impersonal life force and the personal, loving Presence of the heavenly Father.

For several days following, I announced to my students that I'd finally encountered this "living reality." I confessed that I had been wrong in my previous assessment of Ultimate Reality, that I never encountered the true Spirit of God until I went through Jesus, and that consequently, all of my yoga classes would be canceled. Though such an abrupt change was quite shocking to my students, many trusted my insights and enthusiastically opened their hearts to Jesus as well.

I closed the ashram and moved to a Christian mission among the poor migrant workers in Central Florida. In the next few months, many hours were spent studying the Bible and praying—often all night long. It was a season of welcome and wonderful transition, a very important time of learning to discern the difference between incorrect and correct doctrine. As Plato once said, "God is truth, and light His shadow."[7] Because the God of heaven was finally overshadowing me with His personal and gracious influence, the light of truth began to shine more and more with every passing day.

Commentary by Mike Shreve

Just prior to my "transformation," while musing about the differences between the biblical point of view and my New Age belief system—a simple, yet pivotal insight "flashed" in my spirit. It was actually a statement made by my former guru, yet ironically, it caused me to reevaluate the very belief system he had passed on to me. I heard the echo of Yogi Bhajan's voice, insisting:

"Because Jesus was an AVATAR, He could only speak the TRUTH."

It was like someone flipped a spiritual breaker and released a power surge into my mind, causing it to be flooded with light. I immediately sensed the amazing implications of that one sentence.

Basically, an avatar is an incarnation of God, or a god, into fleshly form. According to certain sects of Hinduism and the New Age mindset, there have been many avatars.

I thought to myself, "If this is right, if Jesus was an avatar and could *only* speak the truth, then I'd better inspect His words more closely." To my surprise, as I researched the sayings of Jesus, I began encountering stunning contradictions between what Jesus taught and what Yogi Bhajan and other New Age teachers espoused. For instance—

My guru taught that the birth of Jesus resulted from the normal sexual union of a man and a woman, that Jesus was actually an illegitimate child, and that God could never be so personal as to overshadow a virgin and plant a seed of life within her womb. However, Scripture teaches that Mary *"conceived...of the Holy Spirit"* (Matt. 1:20). Isaiah even prophesied about eight centuries beforehand that a virgin would bear a child and call *"Immanuel"* meaning *God with us* (Isaiah 7:14). So this "lowly Nazarene" was no ordinary man. He was the Son of God. Because of His unique birth, in a far more profound sense than any mere human claiming to be an avatar, Jesus was *"God...manifested in the flesh"* (1 Tim. 3:16). When He referred to God as "His Father," He did not mean it in a general sense, something that all human beings can claim, but in a specific, distinctive and powerful sense. He even declared, *"He who has seen Me has seen the Father"* (John 14:9). "Therefore the Jews sought all the more to kill Him, because He not only broke the Sabbath, but also said that God was His Father, *making Himself equal with God"* (John 5:18). This of itself is a HUGE difference!

My guru taught that there are many paths that lead to God, but Jesus taught just one way. In fact, He maintained, *"I AM THE DOOR. If anyone enters by Me, he will be saved"* (John 10:9). As a yoga teacher, I tried to explain what Jesus *really meant* by that statement—that cultivating His "I AM" consciousness was the door to peace, happiness and self-realization. In other words, seekers must develop an enlightened outlook—the understanding that we are all God and we are all immortal—in order to enter the same level of spirituality Jesus occupied. But that's not what Jesus said. He was very plain in pointing to Himself *personally* as the portal through which everyone must pass in order to be "saved."

In the verse prior He asserted, *"All who came before Me are thieves and robbers"* (John 10:8). "Wow!" I thought, "That would include Lao Tsu, Krishna, Buddha, Zoroaster or any other person who either claimed to be a divine incarnation or a master teacher leading people to Ultimate Reality." I don't think any (who were actual human beings, not mythical) *intentionally* tried to "steal" a position belonging only to Jesus. Most likely, they were all very sincere. However, by claiming to teach ultimate truth, yet misrepresenting the same, they all "robbed" Jesus of His rightful place as the only begotten son of God, the only image of the invisible God.

My guru also taught that Jesus' death on the cross could not redeem anyone from sin; it merely provided an example of obedience—showing each of us how far we should be willing to go in order to fulfill our purpose in this world. However, at the last supper, Jesus passed the cup of wine among His disciples, as He instituted the communion ritual, and prophesied, *"This is My blood of the New Covenant, which is shed for many for the REMISSION OF SINS"* (Matt. 26:28). It's only logical to think that Jesus would be the final authority on the reason behind His own death. He never implied that it was just a model of surrendering to one's destiny; He plainly stated it was for the purpose of "remitting" sin (which means releasing those who have sinned from any resulting guilt or penalties). We know He definitely revealed to His disciples, in advance, that He would die on a cross (see Matt. 16:24; 26:2). If He was prophetically in tune, in advance, with HOW He would die, certainly He also got it right when He told them WHY He would die.

My guru explained that the key to liberation from the cycle of rebirths was to rid oneself of all negative karma and to live a perfect life (self-achieved salvation). Jesus taught an altogether different approach: that through repentance and faith those who come to God can receive forgiveness of sins. He even taught His disciples to pray, *"Father...forgive us our debts as we forgive our debtors..."* (Matt. 6:12). This would mean God, in an ultimate sense, is a *personal God* (just as Jesus taught), not an *impersonal force* (as all my New Age teachers taught). A force doesn't forgive; a person does.

Finally, my guru taught reincarnation. Jesus, on the other hand, taught resurrection. He even prophesied:

170

Do not marvel at this; for the hour is coming in which all who are in the graves will hear His voice [the Messiah's voice] and come forth— those who have done good, to the resurrection of life, and those who have done evil, to the resurrection of condemnation" (John 5:28-29).

He verified this truth, and set a pattern in motion, by rising from the dead Himself, promising, *"Because I live, you will LIVE also"* (John 14:19).

If Jesus was an avatar (and again, I propose that He was the ONLY "avatar" or incarnation of God), and if an avatar can only speak the truth—why did His teachings contradict so many concepts found in Far Eastern religions and New Age spirituality? Back then, I entertained the idea that the Bible had been corrupted, or certain truly inspired books, supportive of a New Age mindset, were passed over by "authorities" who wanted to keep that esoteric knowledge suppressed— but what if that is not the case?

Anyone can do a scholarly study on how we arrived at our present Bible and see the enormous amount of scrutiny that went into its compilation, and how there are very few, mostly minor, differences between the most ancient documents and our modern copies. If the Gospels are the true accounts of Jesus' words (and I believe wholeheartedly they are) then any truth seeker should seriously study them and find out WHAT JESUS ACTUALLY SAID, not just how some guru or teacher interprets what He said.

When I did this, it changed my life. If you dare to do it, it will most likely change yours also.

The word *guru* basically means dispeller of darkness or one who brings you out of darkness into light. If anyone has ever been truly qualified to bear this title and fill this role, it was JESUS. Borrowing that word for a moment, may I say that Jesus is, therefore, the one and only "Great Guru" (Dispeller of Darkness) and only that teaching which agrees with His should be embraced. While on earth, He bolstered this idea with the powerful statement:

"I am the LIGHT OF THE WORLD. He who follows Me shall not walk in darkness, but have the light of life" (John 8:12).

JESUS is even referred to as *"THE TRUE LIGHT,"* so there must be false light as well (John 1:9). So dare to break away from the false. Follow the true Messiah, the true Savior, and darkness will be exiled from your heart and life forever.

Endnotes

1. Huston Smith: The Illustrated World's Religions (New York: HarperCollins Publishers, 1994).

2. http://www.brainyquote.com/quotes/authors/w/william_s_burroughs.html.

3. William Shakespeare, Hamlet, Act 1, Scene V. Quoted at http://www.online-literature.com/shakespeare/hamlet/6/.

4. Elizabeth Barrett Browning, Aurora Leigh, Book vii, no. 6661. Quoted at http://www.bartleby.com/100/446.23.html.

5. The World's Great Religions (New York: Time Incorporated, 1957) p. 38.

6. Thich Nhat Hanh, Living Buddha, Living Christ (New York, New York: Riverhead Books, 1995) p. xvi.

7. http://www.famousquotes.com/show/1007320/.

About the Writer

Mike Shreve, B.Th.,D.D., co-author and editor of this book, has been following the teachings of Jesus since 1970, traveling worldwide to share with others those truth principles from Scripture that bring healing to the whole person. He is the author of ten books, best known for an in-depth comparison of over 20 religions titled, *In Search of the True Light.*

Email: mikeshreve@thetruelight.net

Websites: www.thetruelight.net

www.shreveministries.org

Chapter 8

A True Awakening

By Vail Carruth

*A teacher of Transcendental Meditation
learns the power of the Name of God!*

The University of California Berkeley campus in the 1960s was a place of great social ferment, but some referred to it as "the open ward." Fringe members of the hippie movement like me, and even those from the "far side," found a comfortable social acceptance there. The campus was divided into two main groups at the time: the political activists and the spiritual seekers. Most of us felt that something was terribly wrong with the way things were going in the world. The political activists joined peace marches and student strikes, or served jail time for their confrontations with the police. Those of us who felt we were more "spiritual," or "aware," believed that what the world needed was a transformation in consciousness. We took LSD, smoked grass, went back to the land and joined communes, or meditated.

It seems I was born wanting to know the meaning of life, and my early years were underscored by a deep, relentless hunger for personal identity. My mother, grandmother, and some kitchen helpers told me about the gentle, caring Jesus, and gradually I came to realize God's love for me and His eternal provision through Christ. When I was 12 years old, I responded to a call to invite Jesus into my life. Because I had no mentoring and no understanding of the Bible, this fell short of a life-changing experience. Furthermore, Jesus never seemed very real to me in the church services I attended, and no one ever explained how I could cultivate a personal relationship with Him. The resulting vacuum drew me toward experiences that would prove to be counterfeits of spiritual fulfillment. I thought I could find ultimate answers without a Scriptural basis—an unfortunate mindset held by many in our day.

As I entered my teen years, I became interested in psychic abilities and began dabbling with the Ouija board, astrology, hypnotism, or anything occult. I was fascinated with psychic powers and wanted to learn how to attain them. Consequently, I drifted away from Jesus and more or less "did my own thing." Though I had begun my spiritual journey believing in Jesus as the Messiah, I inevitably cast aside what I perceived as "boring" Christianity and chose the path of mystical self-realization and enlightenment. This pursuit became a near obsession with me, until an event occurred much later that would radically change my life forever.

Hippie Days

Seeking to be closer to where things were really "happening," I moved to the famous Haight-Ashbury section of San Francisco and hung out at the Psychedelic Shop, the famous Bill Graham rock concerts, and the Golden Gate Park Love/Be-Ins. The marijuana and LSD started taking their toll on my memory. I began to view using these drugs as playing Russian roulette with my life and sanity.

Some of my hippie friends taught me the value of health food. They cleared out my entire food pantry declaring almost everything unfit to eat. Out went the white sugar, white flour, white bread, and almost everything else. Within just one day I had switched over to a diet of mostly organic and fresh vegetables, beans, brown rice, honey, and raw food. I came to believe that being high should be the result of a healthy lifestyle and not drugs. The hippies had it right about materialism, but carried it too far, developing a kind of reverse elitism toward anything "establishment." Living in the Haight-Ashbury began to turn sour as reports of thefts and murders surfaced. When the house next door was robbed by a cat burglar, I decided that it was time to move on.

As my interest and experience with altered states of consciousness increased, I began to read many New Age books including the writings of Richard Alpert and Timothy Leary, former Harvard professors who had dropped out of the academic world to pursue the path of altered awareness and spirituality. Berkeley, California, was home to a virtual buffet of spiritual and self-enlightenment groups. When I was not attending classes at the university, I could be found selling my jewelry on Telegraph Avenue, visiting with the street hippies, or hanging out at The Forum coffee shop. Telegraph Avenue was considered the hub of Berkeley's cultural life for many of us.

The writings of Alan Watts and Herman Hesse were very popular at the time, as well as the *I Ching* and *The Tibetan Book of the Dead*. There was a bookstore on Telegraph Avenue called Shambala that featured metaphysical books. I tried to read the *Essene Gospel of Peace*, while my own Bible was gathering dust on a shelf back in my apartment. Whenever someone nudged me to read the Bible, invariably I would begin at Genesis only to get stuck somewhere in the "begets." My spiritual journey might have taken some big steps forward if I had begun with the Psalms, Proverbs, or especially the Gospel of John.

Another Choice

Many times, before making a major shift in my life toward spiritual error, I was mysteriously presented with another viable choice, the "way out"—but I was usually not very responsive. I discovered that two of my acquaintances from college dormitory days were living upstairs in my apartment building. I was amazed to learn that they were the best friends of the head secretary at my job, a former personal secretary of Billy Graham. I met them on the stairs one day, and around their dinner table they shared how they had come to experience a close, personal relationship with Jesus Christ. They described how His love had given them indescribable happiness and peace. They seemed to be enjoying a kind of Christian nirvana, but not spacey like a lot of New Agers I knew. Their joy and fulfillment made me quite jealous, but I just didn't see the answer—though it was right in front of me.

Another Christian was a man who tirelessly preached in front of the Cal Berkeley campus, "Holy Hubert" Lindsey, the original red haired and freckled "Alfalfa" of the TV special, *Our Gang*. Scores of Berkeley hippies and bystanders were converted because Lindsey preached and prayed faithfully in the face of much opposition. Unfortunately, he died many years later, in 2003, partially the result of the many injuries inflicted by his persecutors. God was certainly reaching out to me through these unusual circumstances, but I was unwilling to surrender. The current political correctness was enjoying its infancy in those days. A popular saying was, "Do your own thing as long as it doesn't hurt anyone." I imbibed this attitude and was sold out to the lifestyle and mindset of the sixties.

Even though I had been offered matchless wisdom, all I could see was my own agenda. Faith would have unlocked the golden door to the incredible richness described in Matthew 13:16-17:

But blessed are your eyes for they see, and your ears for they hear; for assuredly, I say to you that many prophets and righteous men desired to see what you see, and did not see it, and to hear what you hear, and did not hear it.

Instead, my friends and I floated on a sea of relativism, refusing to consider the possibility of moral absolutes or doctrinal boundaries—especially anything that breathed normalcy, like the Christian faith. We were not full-fledged hippies, only because we still retained some remnants of decency and social responsibility from our family background. For this moral heritage and for their long-suffering patience, I owe my parents a considerable debt of gratitude.

Transcendental Appeal

When Maharishi Mahesh Yogi, a guru from India, brought transcendental meditation to the United States, it took the Berkeley campus by storm. Disillusioned with drugs as a means to altered awareness, many young people were looking for a safer alternative. We really believed the claim that within five years of practicing TM we would reach enlightenment. We were told that if we became TM teachers our progress would be quicker. The irresistible bait was the promise that such a state of consciousness would free us from all suffering. I swallowed the lure without question.

Unlike regimens requiring hours of concentration or a change of lifestyle, TM's appeal was its easy accommodation to the tempo of modern life. For me, TM promised to meet a need that all the benefits of education and a high standard of living had not fulfilled. And certainly, an undisciplined life had not brought me any closer to knowing who I was. They say hindsight is always perfect. I understand now the hollowness of the claims that were made. It is so much wiser to fully inspect the details before embarking on some new spiritual journey. But then, we were young, idealistic, and impatient for answers.

My first TM experience made me feel very relaxed and high, and I was elated that this could be had without drugs. I was very devoted to my twice daily meditations, attended meetings regularly, and generally enjoyed my life as a meditator. TM was first promoted as a simple means to stress reduction, but it was much more than that. Maharishi announced it as a five-year plan to bliss consciousness. I began to see there was a deep spiritual element pervading every aspect of the practice.

Sproul Plaza on the Berkeley campus was a place where political or spiritual groups could meet and promote their programs. One day I was drawn to a group of Christians who had set up a table in the open square. They seemed to have that "mellow look" that made me think they were meditators. When I asked if they were, they showed me some Scriptures from the Bible I never knew existed—quotes of Jesus like:

"I am the way, the truth, and the life. No one comes to the Father except through Me" (John 14:6).

"All who ever came before Me are thieves and robbers, but the sheep did not hear them" (John 10:8).

This did give me pause to think. These were not the words of some narrow-minded, off-the-wall religious fanatic. They were spoken by Jesus Himself, One respected by adherents of many religions. I began to read my Bible in an effort to find a unity between TM and Christianity, but such effort left me in frustration. So I did the only thing that made sense to me at the time, and that was to put my Bible back on the shelf and to continue TM.

Becoming a TM Instructor

In an effort to speed up my progress toward cosmic consciousness, I enrolled in a teacher-training course in Fiuggi, Italy, directly under Maharishi Mahesh Yogi. There were about 2,000 of us from all over the world. We memorized the TM initiation ceremony in English as well as Sanskrit, and meditated sometimes as much as 12 hours a day. We would "round off" our meditations with breathing exercises, called "*pranayama*," and yoga postures, called "*asanas*."

At this course Maharishi unveiled his "World Plan." His goal was to establish one TM teacher for every 1,000 inhabitants in order to bring about world peace. This would be arranged under the auspices of 8,000 appointed *peace keeping experts* in major cities across the U.S. It might be likened to a spiritual shadow government exerting psychic influence worldwide. It seemed like a plan that would help bring harmony around the globe, but I knew it would only work if we were actually promoting truth.

We teachers were never to teach TM without the *Puja* (the Sanskrit initiation ceremony). Though it was not apparent to newcomers, I eventually discovered it was a worshipful acknowledgment of various Hindu gods and goddesses, as well as TM's honored lineage of gurus. For instance, part of the *Puja* translates:

> To the Lord Narayana, to lotus-born Brahma the Creator, to Vashishtha, to Shakti and his son Parashar, to Vyasa, to Shukadeva, to the great Gaudapada, to Govinda, ruler among the yogis, to his disciple, Shri Shankaracharya, to his disciples Padma Pada and Hasta Malaka and Trotakacharya and Vartika-Kara, to others, to the tradition of our Master, I bow down...offering an ablution to the lotus feet of Shri Guru Dev, I bow down.

Several of the most revered gods in Hinduism are mentioned right at the start: Lord Narayana (another name for Vishnu), Brahma (the creator god) and Govinda (another name for Krishna). Shri Guru Dev was Maharishi's mentor. Unknown to many TM practitioners, during the initiation, a consecration to Hindu deities and a psychic link to the Hindu tradition of departed masters, represented by Maharishi, is established. This required *Puja* is not just a polite ceremony to honor the tradition, which is the explanation normally given.

181

Though it is claimed that TM will make one a better Buddhist, Christian, or any other religion, the philosophy behind the practice of TM still conflicts with the basic values of the Judeo-Christian worldview, as well as other faiths that do not acknowledge these deities or subscribe to their worship. In an earlier book, Maharishi even openly admitted this connection when explaining the mantras TMers are given:

> For our practice, we select only the suitable mantras of personal gods. Such mantras fetch to us the grace of personal gods and make us happier in every walk of life.[1]

It is interesting to note that Jesus taught against the use of *"vain"* or *"meaningless repetitions,"* but instead encouraged His disciples to pray with a fully alert mind in a two-way communication with God through His Spirit (Matt. 6:7 KJV, NASB). This does not involve shutting down the mind or altering the consciousness in any way. Moreover, Jesus passionately upheld the truth of the Ten Commandments, the first of which declared that there is only one God and that none should be worshiped but Him—no gods, no goddesses, no gurus—NONE! How could Jesus be an avatar (one of many incarnations of God) and yet teach things so totally opposite to the New Age belief system? It just seemed impossible to reconcile the two.

At the teacher training course many complained about the negative symptoms they were experiencing, but the leaders said these reactions were merely due to a process of "unstressing." Of course, this explanation was not very convincing or comforting for those going through the distress. We were promised an increase in creativity. However, some studies in the mid 1970s showed that TM might actually decrease creativity in the waking state.[2] More recent investigations have since dismissed these earlier studies, but current efforts to prove the creative effects of TM are often run by TM meditators themselves. Creativity is not easily proven, but from my own observations TM did not make me creative in any productive way.

"Just Ask Them In"

One night an evil spirit tried to take possession of me. This was not a dream or figment of my imagination; it was a real, powerful being with the intention of taking complete control of me. I could feel it putting pressure all over my body, and it was very frightening. Someone asked Maharishi, "What do you do if you see a demon?" to which he replied, "Just ask it in." On another occasion, he conceded that if a demon tries to force itself upon you, resist it and it will leave. So the teaching was not always consistent.

Providentially, I chose to resist. The Hindu tradition does not recognize the very real conflict between good and evil, as the Christian faith teaches. Instead, it is merely explained to be an illusion. Because of my early commitment to Christ, I knew I should resist evil. However, others on the course did not fare so well. One acquaintance of mine told me that she had personal knowledge of an entire wing of a psych ward that was filled with TM practitioners who had flipped out.

After my return from the teacher-training course in Fiuggi, my sense of spiritual emptiness grew. I also observed a lack of love in myself and other meditators. I kept hearing about suicides and divorces, especially among the teachers who had gone in for the longer meditations. I personally witnessed a suicide attempt in the meditators' house where I lived in Berkeley. The woman, who had recently come back from the teacher-training course, was looking for a pair of scissors so she could kill herself. She kept screaming and crying, for a long time. Of course, mental breakdowns such as this can be found among the adherents of many religions, including Christianity—but incidents such as this made me question if I was really using the right methods to achieve lasting peace, mentally, emotionally and spiritually.

Obviously, some of the extreme changes brought about through TM or yoga go far beyond what is referred to as mere "relaxation." Many meditators experienced astral travel, visitation of spirits, psychic awareness, and other manifestations. I began to be "awake" during my sleep state, aware of the beginnings of astral travel. However, I always had a concern—"What would happen if I 'checked out' of my body? Would someone or something else 'check in' while I was gone?" I have since concluded that allowing one's mind to become passive (unattended) is like a country failing to properly guard its borders from foreign invaders. In TM there is something called the *blackout phenomenon* where one goes blank and can't remember anything during that period of time. For me, this virtual "black hole" experience could last anywhere from a few seconds to an hour.

Once someone has been practicing TM for awhile, they are eligible to take the "Yogic Flying" program. Surprisingly, not everyone who takes up this practice belongs to the "lunatic fringe." Some are recognized names in media, business, and politics. The course seemed way too expensive, not to mention ludicrous. No one to my knowledge has ever been able to fly. My original mantra cost $35, but today it can sell for up to $1,500. Advanced techniques can run as much as $100,000. One video course is said to cost a cool million dollars. When Maharishi was asked by someone in his audience how TM would help the poor in India, he responded, "They will be hungry, but they will be happy." The mission Jesus gave to His disciples to feed the hungry and heal the sick provides a strong contrast and a much better solution.

The deeper I went with TM, the more my faith in Jesus just kept getting lost in the archives. Someone once asked me if I was a Christian, because they thought I looked like a believer. I replied that I was not a Christian, but rather a Hindu or a Buddhist. The conditioning process of twice-daily repetition of the mantra had brought about a distancing from my early Christian roots and the embracing of a New Age concept of God as an impersonal energy or force permeating everything. I had turned away from the understanding of God as my Creator, Savior, and Friend.

In spite of my commitment to the goals of TM, however, I saw many things from the inside of the TM movement that I found disturbing. For instance, we were required to hide the Hindu roots and spiritual nature of the practice from the public because ostensibly, most people are not ready for advanced levels of consciousness and would only find it confusing. Therefore, we had to operate by stealth, AKA "the ends justify the means." Every time I presented TM as merely a scientific means to stress reduction, I knew I was lying. One may protest, "Well, I'm just doing TM (or its counterpart Hatha Yoga) for the physical benefits." Sannyasin Arumugaswami, the managing editor of *Hinduism Today,* honestly admits the unavoidable connection. He offers, "Hinduism is the soul of yoga... A Christian trying to adapt these practices will likely disrupt their own Christian beliefs."[3]

Evidently all was not bliss in the ranks of TM meditators, even among those of us who were in the higher echelons. To be honest, the more I continued to practice TM, the more negative character traits I saw in myself. I was becoming increasingly proud, aloof, and insensitive to the needs of others. TM acted as a sort of anesthesia, "numbing down" my conscience and hiding problems that really needed attention. While I was under the illusion that I was becoming a very "evolved" person, the sad truth is that I needed a *change of heart.* As the saying goes, "You can't see the flies in your eyes because you have flies in your eyes." A naïve embracing of the New Age concept of monism (the idea that "all is one") was preventing me from distinguishing simple truth from obvious error.

The Supreme Name

My yearning for spiritual fulfillment eventually caused me to look outside the confines of the TM organization to see what other groups had to offer. Although many people have found transformation through the plain preaching of the Gospel, God chose a nontraditional approach with me. I met a psychic on the Berkeley campus who had dabbled in Christianity. He held some classes, leading us in a unique spiritual practice he described as "Calling on the Name of the Lord."

While I am not recommending this as a correct technique, God used it in my life. First, we were told to tune into the psychic or spiritual fields of spiritual leaders such as Mohammed and Buddha. Then we called upon the names of some friends. Finally he said to call on the name of Jesus, the "Name above all names." He said that God loves us and will respond to our call, as a loving father would respond to his children. He said the Creator would free us from the bondage of the created world. There was a clear distinction between Creator and creation. The Godhead was not to be confused with a "life force," although His power created the world and continues to influence it. So in addition to my silent TM, I called on Jesus making prayerful statements like, "Oh Lord Jesus," "Jesus touch me," "Jesus fill me," "Jesus save me," or simply "Jesus." We were told to call to Him from our heart. It wasn't long before I learned there is incredible power in the Name of the Lord!

After calling on the Name of Jesus for a week, verbally and out loud—not silently like my mantra—my ego began to feel punier and I wondered if I was losing my "psychic abilities" and "higher level of consciousness." I reasoned that the power in this Name was greater than the power of the mantra, so I pressed on and didn't give up even when I felt my foundations shaking. I want to make it clear that I had come to a point in my life where I was willing to do anything to find God! I was willing to lay down all my preconceptions, hopes, and desires, with only one burning desire, to KNOW HIM! God has promised, *"You will seek Me and find Me, when you search for Me with all of your heart"* (Jer. 29:13).

During this time. I often visited with the Hare Krishna group as they sat on the lawn of the Berkeley campus. Their leader (who I felt was a very devout and honest man) told me he thought I was following a deceptive path. He said that the TM organization teaches that

God is already in us, but that their group worshiped Krishna who is separate from human beings. To illustrate his point, he presented an analogy: "Picture a green bird sitting in a green tree. The bird does not become the tree, but remains a bird." It made perfect sense to me. I'd never felt comfortable with the idea that God is an impersonal force anyway. Being a worshiper of God seemed so much truer than wanting to BE God. Anyway, this was closer to the Christian view of being created in the image of God. It's just that I couldn't quite relate to their god, Krishna, represented as a little blue man with a flute. My parents weren't blue, I wasn't blue, and I certainly hoped God wasn't blue.

Transformation

After awhile, the Hare Krishna leader began to read from their sacred Hindu text, *The Bhagavad Gita*. Suddenly he stopped, looked intently at me and said, "You are going to find God because you are sincere." His voice seemed magnified like a megaphone, and something inside of me began to break free. I know this sounds highly unusual, but God can use any means He chooses to reach us with the truth. Then I heard these words from the text: "God has three infinite aspects: Knowledge, Power, and Bliss." I had a burning sense that something of monumental importance was imminent.

Before returning to my apartment, I was standing outside the student union talking with some friends. As I looked across at some trees, I noticed with utter astonishment that somehow they appeared to be clapping their hands in the wind. I did a reality check, and sure enough the trees seemed to be praising God. I was unaware of the Bible verse that says, *"For you shall go out with joy, and be led out with peace; the mountains and the hills shall break forth into singing before you. And all the trees of the field shall clap their hands"* (Isa. 55:12).

Back in my apartment I randomly pulled a book out of the bookcase which fell open to these words, *"God has three infinite aspects: Knowledge, Power, and Bliss."* I was stunned! That night I wanted to commemorate such an amazing day by saying the Lord's Prayer, which in itself indicated a huge change in my life. When I got to the part that says, *"For Thine is the Kingdom, the Power, and the Glory,"* there was a powerful burst of brilliant white light which shook me to the core. Immediately I remembered the words, *"Knowledge, Power, and Bliss."*

The following night I removed all pictures of gurus and spiritual masters from my walls except one: the Lord Jesus. I had concluded that I only needed one Master. This picture was approximately six feet from my bed. Suddenly, there was a knock at the door. My yogi friend stood there and asked if I would join him in calling on the Name of the Lord, as we had done many times before. Shortly after we started, something totally unexpected happened.

The heavenly light of God's inimitable glory descended from above and I felt lifted into a timeless, eternal space. I don't know how long I was in this state, because I lost all sense of time and felt weightless. It was as though I were a child, full of wonder and awe. Cords of bondage, previously unrecognized, were released as wave after wave of the purest, deepest and most indescribable LOVE poured through every fiber of my being. There was a sense of freedom and release that I had never experienced in all my years of TM and yoga. My friend saw this happen to me, but said he did not experience it himself, after which he looked strangely afraid.

When I returned to my bedroom, the picture of Jesus had amazingly been changed to a different location, right beside my pillow. Suddenly, I was thrust into a vision of something like a flaming dart piercing my heart again with this love that was unconditional, permanent, and totally undeserved. This amazing love changed me forever. By placing this picture next to my pillow, God was sending me the undeniable message that He had drawn me close and that He is the Friend who will always *"stick closer than a brother"* (Prov. 18:24). I knew I had a secure relationship with Him that nothing could take away.

Compass of Life

As a result of this breakthrough, the Word of God (the Bible) became a compass of spiritual direction and living inspiration for me. The TM mantra no longer held the same power or attraction. Instead, it brought negative results, so I stopped. The power of Jesus and His precious name threw light on everything dark and sinful in my life, and His love truly set me free!

Ironically, though I had looked disdainfully on them in the past, I too became a "Jesus freak" in the eyes of others. Humbled, but undaunted, I relished every opportunity to share Jesus with the misguided and wandering souls where I lived. I did go through what I refer to as my "white period" in which I wore beads and white clothes because I thought they had pure vibes. I didn't realize that outward trappings don't have a thing to do with inward purity. Nevertheless, God used it to disarm a lot of spiritual seekers who otherwise would have kept a "safe" distance from me.

During this time, a friend of mine and I visited some ashrams and yoga centers. We asked them if they would like to experience Jesus for themselves. Most of the time, they responded favorably. After all, they called on the names of gods and spirit guides all the time. It shouldn't be considered too strange to call on the One who claimed to be the Creator manifested in human form. Several of them were radically changed.

Gradually, I came to understand the difference between true salvation and cosmic consciousness. I was able to differentiate between authentic spiritual gifts and counterfeit psychic manifestations. But Jesus did not disappoint my desire for the supernatural! Right from the start of this new life, I experienced many divine touches and miracles of God, including a dramatic, fully documented healing of my own spine. Of course, the greatest miracle of transformation occurred in the sanctuary of my heart. For this I am eternally grateful.

There is no greater way of summing up this account than to quote an appropriate passage from my compass, the Bible:

The Lord says, "I will rescue those who love Me. I will protect those who trust in My name. When they call on Me, I will answer; I will be with them in trouble. I will rescue and honor them. I will reward them with a long life and give them My salvation" (Psalms 91:14-16 NLT).

Commentary by Mike Shreve

The key element in Vail's transformation was calling on the Name of the Lord. This is a very important point. Of course, there are many seekers who say, "It doesn't matter. Regardless of what name a person uses for God, He is still being worshiped." There was a time when I would have vigorously upheld this view without qualification. But then I realized my error.

We associate any name with the one who bears it—and the mention of that name brings to mind the character (or lack of it) the named person possesses. And so it is with our concept of God. Krishna is considered the Supreme Being by many of his followers. According to Hindu lore, Krishna married 16,108 women and had ten children by each of them over a span of 125 years. Supposedly, he expanded himself into 16,108 forms so he could live in a palace with each of his wives.

If this is not true (and it certainly isn't), then if God responded to the name Krishna in a supernaturally real way, He would be validating an untrue myth and making a very confusing statement about Himself. Furthermore, He would be verifying the doctrines promoted by Krishna in Hindu literature (which includes concepts like reincarnation, karma, and the divinity of humankind).

Consider two other examples:

In the Muslim faith, God is referred to as "Allah." He is considered so absolutely "One" that associating divinity with anyone or anything is considered the highest of sins, called *shirk*. Based on this, in Islam, it is considered blasphemy to say that Jesus was the *"Son of God"* or *"God manifested in the flesh"* (Luke 1:35, 1 Tim. 3:16). The biblical view concedes that yes, there is only ONE GOD, but enhances that truth with the understanding that He is triune in nature: Father, Son, and Holy Spirit. These two views of the Godhead are completely irreconcilable. So evidently, if God responded in a supernaturally real way to the name Allah, He would be denying His own triune nature. [4]

In Hinduism, Ultimate Reality is Brahman, an impersonal energy force, or cosmic level of consciousness. "Impersonal" means a nonhearing, nonseeing, noncommunicative, nonresponsive cosmic power. Hindus do not pray to Brahman for Brahman does not answer; instead, they meditate on Brahman as an internal, divine life-essence. It is important to note that within Brahman there is both darkness and light, both good and evil.

The true God is a personal God who comprehends and deeply senses all our needs, who hears our appeals to Him and a God in whom is NO darkness or evil. If God responded to the name Brahman, He would be verifying that "He" is actually an "It": no more than a universal "force" and that the true nature of Ultimate Reality is a mix of both good and evil (as the yin-yang symbol indicates).

However, when we call on the name of JESUS, we automatically associate that name with the essence of who He was and what He did: how He has always existed as the *"image of the invisible God,"* how he was born of a virgin (the ONLY incarnation of GOD), how He lived a sinless life, was crucified for our sins, yet victoriously arose, conquering death (Col. 1:15). We also associate that name with the doctrines of the Bible—including the belief that there is only one life in this world and one way to salvation.

Certainly, there are many seekers in this world who truly and deeply love God, yet when they pray, they call on various names that God has not applied to Himself, and often those names are associated with nonbiblical stories, myths, and legends. They may be "worshipers," but they are not yet *true worshipers* (John 4:23). As mentioned in an earlier commentary, Jesus taught that only those who "worship in spirit and in truth" qualify for this status—and part of "worshiping in the truth" involves uttering the true name of God when we call on Him. If you have never done it before, try calling on the name of JESUS (or the Hebrew equivalent: YESHUA) until He responds. Don't do it in a monotone, mantra-like way, but a loving, worshipful, prayerful way.

It worked for Vail, and it will certainly work for you.

You have nothing to lose and everything to gain.

Endnotes

1. Maharishi Mahesh Yogi, Beacon Light of the Himalayas, 1955.

2. Colin Martindale, "Creative People: What Makes Them So Different," Psychology Today (July 1975), p. 50.

3. Quoted in Darryl E. Owens, "A New Wave of Christian Yoga," Knight Ridder News Service, June 1, 2006, www.religionnewsblog.com/14838/a-new-wave-of-christian-yoga. Original quote from Orlando Sentinel, May 14, 2006.

4. Ironically, Jesus is actually called the "Word of God" and "the Spirit of God" in the Quran, which are entitlements that indicate His deity (Surah 4:171). Also, the pronoun "We" is used when God speaks in the Quran, just as in the Bible. (Surah al-Anbiya' 21:107). Again there is only ONE GOD, but He is triune in nature.

About the Writer

Vail Carruth holds a BA in Fine Arts from the University of California, Berkeley, and studied piano at the San Francisco Conservatory of Music. Vail is also an artist, a dream interpreter, and the author of a powerful book on her spiritual journey, *Authentic Enlightenment*. Her sole desire is to exalt her Creator and to make Him known to others.

Email: vail@living-light.net

Website: www.living-light.net

Chapter 9

Secret Realms and Secret Doors

By Dr. Jean LaCour

*A political activist turns to yoga, Rosicrucianism,
Magick, and mountaintop communal living
projects, then finds the higher Way!*

It was a cold weekend in January of 1966 when my best friend and I visited her older cousin in another town. We were 16. She was undeniably cool. Her room was painted dark turquoise blue. We drank malt liquor and smoked cigarettes. She taught us how to blow smoke rings while we listened to *Highway 61 Revisited* on her record player. I was truly unprepared for what happened next.

Bob Dylan's throaty voice gripped me totally in that dark, smoky room: "*There's something happenin' here and you don't know what it is, do you, Mr. Jones?*" That throbbing, jagged chorus was a potent and pivotal moment for me. I felt like I was being pulled into a hallway with many doors. Something was beckoning me to enter and in my heart, I "stepped in." I *knew* there was something "out there" beyond my five senses, but I didn't have words for it. Then this spiritual shift happened inside of me. It left me yearning for more.

I found a valid explanation in *The Aquarian Conspiracy* by New Age author Marilyn Ferguson. She noted that my type of experience was a hallmark among thousands who surfaced into New Age consciousness and identified it as a *Point of Entry,* or P.O.E. I finally had words. My experience was an initiation into a spiritual realm. According to Ferguson, P.O.E. catalysts include drug experiences and other consciousness-raising techniques like meditation, yoga, chanting, visualization, certain intense therapies, or transcendent moments.

Ferguson described this life-changing, perceptual phenomenon as a paradigm shift in consciousness. *Reality* literally shifts along with our worldview, which is the *map* we use unconsciously to define what is *real to us* and *who we are* in our reality. This can happen suddenly or gradually. We can seek this shift or it can be "offered" to us unexpectedly. Our will must come into agreement on some level. In *Doors of Perception,* Aldous Huxley spoke about *seeing* in an entirely new way. He encouraged true seekers to search for these doors. He didn't mention that if we attempt to enter these doors, without true divine guidance, it could lead to confusion and insanity—conditions, unfortunately, that I have personally witnessed, far too often.

It was over 16 years before I learned how to fully disengage from the supernatural beings that called me into their realm that dark cold night. Only the purest love can produce the supernatural power needed to wisely navigate the realm of the supernatural, and I was yet to meet the Source of that unfailing love.

In essence, a "point of entry" opens a person's consciousness to spiritual realms. Once I experienced the supernatural realm and sensed its "wonders," I was fascinated. It was easy to assume that this was the Kingdom of Heaven of which Jesus spoke so often—but it wasn't (see Matt. 4:17; 5:3; 13:11).

Rather, it was like preferring a dark back alley to the splendor of a mansion, or eating garbage when I was invited to a wondrous feast. Not everything that glitters is gold. I settled for shiny beads when precious gems were my inheritance. But how was I to know the difference? Science told theology to close the ancient books on spiritual wisdom. Our rational worldview turned us into lambs among lurking wolves.

The dark feelings I experienced in this realm made it necessary to find a guide, master, mantra or technique to help me "navigate" and raise my consciousness back to the "light." Ancient knowledge of spirit guides is found in Eastern religions, Native American and Indian practices, in metaphysical secret societies that tap Ascended Masters, in shamanism and witchcraft. It seemed my guides always appeared when I was spiritually ready: most susceptible and vulnerable to their influence.

Departing Faith / 1967

I actually struggled to hold onto my childhood faith. I loved God. I sang in children's choir in our historic Episcopal church. I experienced His presence through reverent ritual and worship, but I didn't have a biblical grasp of the Gospel message. Furthermore, I had this deep longing in my heart for some faraway "secret place" that I didn't really understand.

At the time, a cultural battle was also raging. I can still see *Time* from April 1966 with its stark black cover and shocking red letters that asked, "Is God Dead?" Eloquent theologians asserted modern secularism had totally done away with earlier concepts of God. America was so advanced and prosperous due to scientific breakthroughs that faith in God had become irrelevant or archaic. Methodist seminary students in Atlanta published an *Obituary for God* saying He'd died during the surgery that was meant to correct His diminishing influence. Who was I to argue?

But I had to ask someone. I chose my respected head minister. At 17, I didn't know how to frame questions about the meaning of life or church doctrine. What I really wanted to ask was why I had fantastic dreams of flying, saw lights around people, and heard an inner voice. And why did I just *know things* about people? Invisible things… Was I psychic or crazy? Did Christians believe in being psychic? I must have asked the wrong questions, because he just gave me a book by a baffling theologian and exited from the conversation. It chilled my heart to realize he had no answers for me.

Before I left home for college I went into the beautiful sanctuary where I'd grown up. I tearfully thanked God for so many good things, but said goodbye to Him with a heavy heart. Christianity seemed to belong to political conservatives like my mother, and liberal intellectuals didn't want it. I didn't see how I fit in anymore. I admitted I was a rule breaker and the road ahead was likely filled with more unacceptable behavior, so I knew it was over. I couldn't be a hypocrite. My understanding was very clear: first you behave, then you can belong, then *somehow* you get to believe. I had failed at the "behaving" part badly.

Psychedelic Possibilities / 1968

The cover of *LIFE* magazine on March 25, 1966, proclaimed, "Turmoil in a Capsule—One dose (of LSD) is enough to set off a mental riot of vivid colors and insights or of terror and convulsions." The article described someone's fantastic experience of "taking a trip" on LSD.

Reading that article convinced me I had to "drop acid." I believed it would guide me back to the gateway into the unknown territory and the *secret* things I yearned for.

In early 1968, I visited a friend at Florida State University in Tallahassee. She introduced me to Charles, who would become the love of my life. I'd never seen a person with so much light coming through his face. When I told my friend what I saw, she thought I was crazy. There were always lots of drugs around in those days. We liked pot and speed. When someone gave me four hits of LSD, I shared them with Charles.

All I can say is, *LIFE* did not exaggerate. On that unforgettably intense morning when we first dropped acid, I *heard* a flower sing and *felt* my parents' love. I *saw* the floating colors of music and *knew* the world could be healed. Charles and I *walked for eons* it seemed across the campus with fantastic adventures at every corner and crack in the sidewalk. We lost one of the trippers who went off on his own. He ended up at a hospital emergency room so he could come down.

But I never planned to come down. I was convinced that the doors of perception were thrown wide open, and I was getting closer to that *knowing*—touching a power source I assumed was altogether good and pure. During the next two years I dropped acid over *one hundred* times. It's a miracle I kept my sanity and finished college, given the summer of 1968 in Haight-Ashbury and hitchhiking the California coast tripped out. I didn't think about the risks, just the *possibilities*.

One vivid, terrifying experience happened the night I saw *Rosemary's Baby* while on LSD. In the movie, Mia Farrow's sweet character and her husband are manipulated by a coven of witches who deceive her into having sex with the devil for a night. She gives birth to a diabolical infant, which they take from her. Later, I returned to the old house where I was staying in West Hollywood. I was too frightened to sleep and desperately searched the L.A. phone book trying to find a minister who would talk to me in the middle of the night. No one answered my calls. I *had to know* if Episcopalians believed in satan. By dawn, I calmed down enough to convince myself that no rational person believed in such a supernatural force or persona of evil.

The summer of 1969, I hitched with an ever-changing band of international youth intent on cruising high through all the countries of Europe. From Stonehenge in England to the canals of Venice, I rolled on—seeking something illusive.

It's not easy to describe the sense of belonging, rightness, and movement that marked the shifting migration and melding of young people from California to India in those days. Woodstock was real. Like characters in James Michener's novel *The Drifters*, we were a tribe, a clan, a "nation" fueled by a heady mixture of flawed idealism, psychedelics, and a burden for civil rights, equality, and an end to war. And every waking moment was intensified by the constant beat of fantastic music—music created to alter consciousness. Our music hinted that utopia was possible even as our epic bards died of drug overdoses.

I understand now that I was addicted to the actual "trance state" of hallucinogenic drugs just like my friends who were physically addicted to drugs like heroin. We were all "hooked" once we repeatedly overwhelmed the pleasure center in our brains. I have also realized after many years that people can become "psychic junkies" as well, from the euphoric recall inherent in point-of-entry experiences and from potent, spiritual disciplines that don't involve drug use. Neuropathways in the brain are developed by repetition—and our "tribe" certainly excelled at this: *repeating* certain *excessive* behavior patterns over and over again!

Political Panic / 1969

College equaled *political* intensity—in the 1960s especially. I majored in political science. My other passion was history with a focus on twentieth century Soviet studies. The Cold War was raging; it was not make believe.

University of South Florida in Tampa had its share of radical professors. At 18, I was hit by the lightning of political activism and the painful realities of the times. Boys from my high school were already coming home in bodybags from Vietnam: sweet boys, good boys. My only brother was being deployed as a highly trained Army combat pilot flying Cobra gunships. Civil rights struggles were intensifying in Tampa's ghettos. A friend was arrested during a dangerous, botched abortion.

Nothing was abstract! It was all up close and personally painful. My soul ached with friends thrown out by angry parents, the drug overdoses and arrests, the racial violence, young men who were AWOL or maimed from war. We'd seen the blood of our slain heroes a hundred times on TV: JFK in 1963; Martin Luther King Jr. and Bobby Kennedy in 1968.

Yet I still believed in the political process to bring change. At the urging of a professor friend, I transferred in 1969 to the University of Massachusetts in Amherst for my junior year. Students had been shot in Ohio by National Guardsmen and young protesters had been violently arrested in Chicago. In November, I was one of 500,000 people who went to Washington for a massive Moratorium to End the War. Our group was intent on reaching a specific federal building when the tear gas began!

Our peaceful group became an angry, vicious mob—a boiling rage surged through me and I wanted to destroy our attackers. I had become just like the violent racists and brutal police I'd seen on TV. I was horrified! We were no different! Our cause had descended into a hate-filled battle. True nonviolence requires spiritual leadership that we didn't have. Martin Luther King Jr. was really dead. A new breed known as Black Panthers was waiting in the wings. I couldn't allow myself to go there.

I don't remember how I made it across the city to find my ride back to Amherst. I was in a disoriented daze, not just from tear gas but from profound disillusionment that settled into months of depression. As New England got colder and darker, I decide to go back to the warmth of Tampa to regain my footing. I was finished with politics and even more desperate for *peace*.

Pondering My Breath / 1970

I returned to Tampa in early 1970 and embraced the peaceful solace in *nature*. Canoeing the Hillsborough River soothed my weary mind, while gardening nourished my body. Charles reentered my life in his Volkswagen camper and we set off for Boca Raton, where he began graduate school in mathematics at Florida Atlantic University while I waitressed. Seeking a new type of *natural high,* I took my first yoga class at a community center.

My yoga teacher called me Carol. When I corrected her, she claimed she knew me as Carol in a former life and said I needed to join her at a nearby *ashram* (Hindu religious center) to pursue mastery. Hatha Yoga was as natural as breathing for me—it was *living* my breath.

She gave me a book on mysticism and said Jesus was one of the great avatars who had reached the highest level of spiritual consciousness. He came to show us how to realize our own divine potential. Her words brought to mind my visits to the meditation gardens at the S.R.F. Center (Self Realization Fellowship) in Los Angeles two summers earlier. On the altar in their chapel I saw portraits of the great spiritual masters side by side: Buddha, Krishna, Moses, Mohammed— and there was Jesus, looking serene among His peers.

On my first visit to the ashram, the guru, Ma Yogashakti, had just arrived from India to work with her followers. Doing *asanas* and *pranayama* (physical postures and breathing) under her direction quickened my inner senses. Her eyes were pools of black intensity that laid bare my very soul.

With chanting came a sense of *peace*, like going into a quiet alcove off a noisy corridor. I could return there by choice. I learned disciplines designed to undo my negative karma (consequences) and my attachment to the illusion of separateness and to deconstruct my ego/self and release my desires that held me back from union with God.

Perfection meant actually "becoming" God, like a raindrop falling into the ocean and merging into its vastness. No more disturbing cross or Pearly Gates to contend with.

I was invited to move into the ashram to serve Ma Yogashakti and accompany her to local speaking engagements at the Theosophical Society, Unity churches, and other New Age venues. She began to teach me Sanskrit as we translated her booklets on yoga. It was a strict and formal relationship. Before she left, she opened the door for me to move to India and formalize our master/disciple relationship. Only my love for Charles kept me from leaving the country with her. I wasn't completely ready to forsake all for the spiritual path that beckoned so strongly.

Pursuing the Antelope / 1971 to 1973

Early in 1971, Charles and I moved back to Tampa. In the spring I finished my BA and we were married. We entered a graduate program to train "culturally disadvantaged" children. It involved social justice and gave us skills we'd need in a communal setting.

A tidal wave was moving through the counterculture that swept many of us into communes. The next five years, we were totally immersed in going "back to the land": to create self-sufficient communities as a positive political/moral action.

During grad school we prepared to move to British Columbia and live off the land. For two years, we teamed up with a disillusioned Vietnam veteran and his girlfriend. His brand of "Special Forces intensity" was demanding. We spent the first winter together in a nonwinterized cabin outside of Casper, Wyoming.

I learned to shoot a rifle, reload shells, can antelope meat, and tan the hides in a barrel. By midwinter of 1973, we were exhausted from the extreme cold, hard work, and group dynamics. Charles, who is ultimately a man of peace, agreed it was time to pack our truck and set off. During our trek, my sense of failure was growing, along with a deep emptiness. Charles suggested I go to an ashram to get my *peace* back. So we headed to Daytona Beach for him to get a job and I took off for an ashram in the Caribbean.

Paradise Island Surrender / 1973

Entering the lush tropical surroundings of the Sivananda Yoga Ashram on Paradise Island brought about a deep reconnection as my body and my breath became one again in fluid motion. I tasted my destiny in meditation, fasting, and chanting—as I traded my long blond hair for a "crew cut" and rested in the repose of a spiritual seeker. Swami Vishnu-devananda had created a welcoming environment for reflection.

I was at a crossroads. In order to go through the open door in India and work with my guru, I would have to surrender everything. With conscious intention, I must lay down family, friends, and heritage in order to release my *negative karma* (the consequences resulting from every thought, attitude, and action) and experience "union with God."

Sitting in lotus posture in deep meditation in exquisite tropical beauty, I came to the realization that I was profoundly lost. I knew I *must* have the help of a spiritual master to burn off my past deeds and help me progress spiritually. Thinking of India, I became acutely aware I did not really know my own spiritual heritage; in order to sacrificially leave it behind I needed to know its value. A piercing thought entered my mind: Jesus was a stranger to me. I only knew what others said about Him. In that moment I *had to know Him*, my life depended on it. From my deepest self I asked, "JESUS... WHO ARE YOU, *REALLY*?" An overwhelming peace flooded my soul. I knew an answer would come.

It was indeed another point of entry, a profound shift. Something eternal had happened. A door had opened. I would be able to leave my former life behind and step into my destiny. I was being guided into deeper consciousness.

Two months later I went to see my mother in St. Augustine. We visited our home church where I'd said goodbye to God six years earlier. During the first hymn, a dazzling and brilliant light broke through the familiar stained glass window over the altar. Out of that amazing light He SPOKE to me saying, "Jean, I AM the Way...out of karma." Under the law of karma (negative consequence), I knew I couldn't measure up. I saw no way out of the wheel of endless futility and rebirth. The words Jesus spoke were the most comforting words in the universe! There was indeed a way out of my dreadful confusion from the untruths about karma and having many lives. My efforts could never perfect me; He died for me so I could LIVE and have union with Him now!

I was stunned, flooded with joy and amazement! He was real. He knew my name and understood my despair. How I longed to jump up, shout, and sing—but we Episcopalians keep very quiet, so the moment was mine alone. The experience was quite dramatic, but oddly, it would be years before I understood its profoundness and the exclusiveness of the One who spoke.

Power Pursuits and Psychotic Breaks / 1973 to 1975

Our plans to depart for India were delayed as Charles and I joined friends on a 140-acre backwoods commune in western North Carolina. We lived there a full year with no power or plumbing as we stockpiled food and supplies. We waited for the Comet Kohoutek to appear in the skies over *The Late Great Planet Earth*. Our little group could not foresee how desperately we would need true spiritual power in the darkness ahead.

Charles and I disappeared into a "parallel universe" when we hiked up that steep, rugged mile to what appeared to be a peaceful mountain farm. The "gifted" leader named John was definitely into power. From *The Teachings of Don Juan: A Yaqui Way of Knowing* by anthropologist Carlos Castaneda, we learned about spirit guides and his partial initiation into "nonordinary reality." As a classic sorcerer, Don Juan guided him in using peyote (mescaline) and other plants sacred to the Mexican Indians as gateways into supernatural mysteries like *clarity* or *power* or *dread*. Each drug manifested a unique "spirit being" that Castaneda had to discern and work with. Don Juan referred to these familiar beings as his *allies*. We sought after allies as well, hoping for the same kind of "enlightenment."

I have since learned that ancient Jewish and Christian scriptures forbid humans to invoke or interact with demonic forces (disembodied spirits) like this. The Greek word for "sorcerer" is *pharmakeus,* from which we get the word "pharmacy" where drugs are dispensed—so the connection between sorcery and mind-altering drugs is clearly exposed. Sorcerers and necromancers (those who profess to call up the dead to answer questions) are described as having a "familiar spirit." This is the biblical term for spirit guides (see Deut. 18:11; 2 Kings 21:1-9; Lev. 19:31; 20:6,7; Isa. 8:19; 29:4). According to Easton's Bible Dictionary, the word "familiar" is from the Latin word *familiaris,* meaning a "household servant." It expressed the idea that sorcerers had spirits as their servants (or "allies") ready to obey their commands.

The Hebrews called a sorcerer an *owb,* which refers to a bottle made from leather, because such persons were regarded as vessels containing a spirit that brought a false kind of *inspiration* (see Lev. 20:27; 1 Sam. 28:8). In the New Testament, the story is shared about a woman who was possessed with a "spirit of divination," who brought her masters much money through her demonically inspired "soothsaying" (fortune telling). The Greek word for divination is *pytho* (which relates to the Greek god Pythias, or Apollos, the god of prophecy). Notice the connection to the constrictive snake, the python. This demon was discerned and cast out by Paul, the apostle (see Acts 13:6-12; 16:16-18). In New Age terminology, a person under this kind of supernatural influence is called a channeler.

Jesus taught that no person can serve two masters—but we were trying hard to do that very thing: mixing darkness with light and the power of satan with the power of God (see Matt. 6:24). It's a miracle we survived.

We also implemented the teaching of occultist Aleister Crowley, who taught in his books on "Magick" that all such work must begin with the body and breath control of classic yoga. My ashram experience finally had practical application. John and I also entered a kind of time/space/power warp through a sequence of metaphysical initiations we obtained from yet another group: the AMORC, the Ancient Mystical Order Rosae Crusis, or Rosicrucian Society. Their esoteric heritage is based on the ancient mystery schools of Egypt.

After specific vows, we were called students and received monographs through the mail. We carefully practiced exercises such as focusing our mental concentration to move a needle floating on water. We took part in raising the consciousness of mankind by focusing our thoughts toward the "Celestial Sanctum," which is supposedly a spot in the universe outside of time and space. We were told to visualize a magnificent cathedral where we'd gather in the psychic realm. Rosicrucians from across the globe collectively focus their thoughts for world peace or harmony according to detailed instructions based on latitude, longitude, and time zone on the exact window of time in order to synchronize with others praying for the good of the planet or for a specific world leader or event.

We thought these were very positive and legitimate involvements, but one very dark night I discovered otherwise. I was walking up the steep wooded path to our lean-to and suddenly realized I was surrounded by malevolent beings (evil spirits). In a panic, I screamed out the name of Jesus… in a swirling rush the entities vanished! Stillness filled the air. I learned that when I couldn't handle it, I could call to *Jesus* and He would *help* me. I considered Him *my* Master, even though there was still a considerable amount of deception in my life.

Over time, the psychic distress mounted as more intimidating supernatural entities showed up and insane melodrama took over. In the end, our false spiritual practices, the pressure of drugs, and communal living led to psychotic breaks and violence. Eventually John committed suicide. Our love wasn't strong enough to hold him, and our so-called "spiritual wisdom" came from polluted streams.

After things settled down, we came off that mountain and moved into an old farm nearby to "detox" spiritually and emotionally. For two more years, we grew our food and helped our neighbors. Charles became a social worker. We were much at home in the friendly overlap of our counterculture friends and the long-time farm families of rural Appalachia. Our first child was born and brought much joy into our lives. To pay for the 50 acres, we decided to make a temporary move to Florida. Little did I know that everything was about to change.

Prodigal Path / 1976

Not all transitions are smooth. Mine wasn't. For ten years I had wandered down alternate spiritual paths. It took months to find my way back. I knew it was time to connect with people who truly knew Jesus. I'd heard about a Christian group meeting in a house and agonized for weeks about going. Knowing the power of concealment and invisibility, I was very distressed about how to proceed. Should I wear pants or a skirt? Lipstick or no? Carry a Bible or not?

I figured I could get into the house, but didn't know what kind of power I would face. My fear was that they would know I didn't *belong*. I sat back in a corner and listened as a man read from the Bible,

Behold! My Servant whom I uphold, My Elect One in whom My soul delights! I have put My Spirit upon Him...A bruised reed He will not break...He will bring forth justice for truth... I, the Lord, have called You in righteousness....As a light to the Gentiles...to open blind eyes, to bring out prisoners from the prison...I am the LORD, that is My name; **And My glory I will not give to another...** (Isaiah 42:1,3,6,7,8, emphasis by author).

Each word went through me like quicksilver! I understood what God was saying. He had given His glory to Jesus, the Messiah, *ALONE!* He was not one of many! I'd never heard these things. My mind was swirling. They *had* to let me come back, or despair would overcome me. Thankfully, a kind person extended that invitation. I didn't go regularly until I felt more at ease with their spiritual protocols. But little by little, I changed.

As I learned more truth and absorbed *life* from the Scriptures, I closed the last of the doors I'd thrown open. I learned to say no to the deceptive spirit beings that came with false spiritual experiences. I began to appreciate and celebrate the uniqueness of Jesus. He is unlike all other gods, gurus, and spiritual entities! His beauty and majesty are wrapped in gentleness and patience. He is closer than our next breath—ever waiting for us to return to His love.

The Living Eternal Portal

We all have access to the supernatural realm. I think of it like another country. We can enter legally or illegally. We can stealthily crawl across a border in the night or be concealed in a clandestine vehicle driven by someone with a scheme to "help us." We can accidently stumble across a border that is not clearly marked. But when we enter another country *illegally,* we become *vulnerable.* Foreigners with no legal standing are vulnerable targets. We don't know who is trustworthy or what we will encounter. There is no peace.

When we enter another country *legally,* it is because we are *known.* Proof of our birth and citizenship are recorded in our passport, a legal document with an official seal. Legal entrance guarantees us rights, privileges, and protection, and results in a peaceful sojourn.

I've learned there is only *one* legal entrance into the supernatural realm, and He calls Himself "*The Door*" (John 10:9). He is Pure Light— "*The Light of the World*" (John 9:5). When you accept His invitation, walk through the "Door," and enter the "Light," you can rest assured, you will be welcomed.

Those who enter the realm of the Holy Spirit through the legal Entrance are spiritually reborn. They are "sealed" (marked) by the Holy Spirit as God's own. Because of His fiery love toward us, His off-spring receive certain rights, privileges, and protection as true heirs. This "initiation" into God's Kingdom reveals "*the mystery of God*"— both the Father and the Messiah—"*in whom are hidden all the treasures of wisdom and knowledge*" (Col. 2:2-3). All the deep insights I sought for are found in Him. Now He is waiting for you. Come to Him and you will be filled with Pure Light. He will arise in your heart like the dawning of a new day.

Commentary by Mike Shreve

Jean's amazing and heart-warming story is all about her discovery of the right "portal" or "point of entry" into the supernatural realm. This is surely the primary motivation for many who are disenchanted with mere *religion* (be it Buddhism, Christianity, Judaism, Hinduism, or otherwise) and impassioned to discover reality—Ultimate Reality.

But why is it that Jean concluded, as others in this book, that there is only one path—ONE TRUE DOOR—that leads a seeker into a correct experience of the highest "dimension of existence"? Consider the following explanation.

In the Bible, Paul talks about "three heavens" (see 2 Cor. 12:2). The "first heaven" is the lowest—it is the physical "heaven": the atmosphere that surrounds this planet, as well as the starry cosmos beyond. The "third heaven" is the highest, synonymous with "paradise," the realm of the manifest Presence of GOD and absolute perfection. But what are the characteristics of the mysterious, intermediate sphere known as the "second heaven"?

This "second heaven" is a bridge between the lower and upper realms (which are not "stacked" but "concentric"—just like human beings who are composed of body, soul, and spirit, yet these three parts occupy somewhat the same "space"). Apparently, the second heaven is filled with spiritual activity, both angelic and demonic. Satan is described biblically as *"the prince of the power of the air,"* but he is not seen visibly moving about in the actual atmosphere (Eph. 2:2). Rather, he and his demonic underlings move about in the realm just above our natural perception, yet they constantly seek to express themselves in this earthly sphere. The only "legal" way they can do that is by manipulating, possessing, or "channeling" themselves through human beings who are susceptible to their influence (see Ps. 115:116).

When truth seeking individuals open themselves up to the spiritual world (through chanting mantras, meditating on chakras, focusing on yantras, participating in séances, psychic experimentation, Ouija boards, or other incorrect methods), they succeed, at times, in penetrating this realm. However, because of the dark entities resident there, deception is inevitable for those who are unprotected—those who are not truly saved and sealed by the Holy Spirit. Satan can even *"transform himself into an angel of light"* and so can the demons under his charge (2 Cor. 11:14). They will gladly impart all kinds of false "spiritual" encounters to those who enter their domain—in order to keep such "spiritual explorers" from ever knowing the ONE TRUE GOD. I am convinced that the "out-of-body astral trips" and even the "white light" I encountered during my time of practicing Kundalini

Yoga were deceptive, counterfeit experiences in this very realm. I feel certain that these encounters were not merely "imaginary" experiences; they were real, supernatural, soulish happenings, but usually misleading.

Because all human beings are stained with sin and separated from God, none can legally enter the third heaven to experience true communion with God by his or her own will (see Isa. 59:2). That realm is blocked to us. There is a supernatural firewall we can't pass through. But here is the key—the One who dwells in that realm can *come to us*. And that is exactly what happened in the incarnation. Jesus descended to earth and dared to say, *"No one has ascended to heaven but He who came down from heaven, that is, the Son of Man who is in heaven"* (John 3:13). What an astounding statement! Anyone speaking such profound words would necessarily have to be insane, a full-blown egotist, a religious liar, *or* a "True Witness" pointing the way to restored relationship with the Creator. Surely the latter is the only possible answer!

Why do we have to go through Jesus (Yeshua)? Because there are unique things about Him that no one else can match. Mohammed was not born of a virgin. Buddha did not live a perfect life. Krishna did not die on the cross for the sins of the human race. And none of them rose from the dead. All of these things not only demonstrate the uniqueness of Jesus; they reveal His deity.

All religions and methods of spirituality are merely man's attempt to reach God; Jesus is God's attempt to reach man. Even the most spiritual, religious person, given to supernatural sensitivity, can only penetrate the second heaven—but Jesus came *"from above,"* from the third heaven (John 8:23). So He alone can grant entrance into that realm. This cannot happen through chanting some secret mantra, a guru's touch, or by bathing in the river Ganges—it can only happen by being *"born again"* (the Greek *anothen*, literally means "born from *above*"— John 3:3). This occurs when repentant and believing persons invite the Lord Jesus into their hearts. They are then washed and made pure by the precious blood that He shed and indwelt by the Spirit of God. From that point forward their God-given right is to dwell in "*heavenly places in Christ*" (Eph. 2:6).

Only those who personally experience this supernatural reality understand how radically different it is from the spiritual experiences offered through other religious practices. Only those who experience the reality of the third heaven understand how far it transcends any lower realms. Sincere prayer will take you there. Try it. Call on the name of Jesus. You will not be disappointed.

About the Writer

Dr. Jean LaCour is co-founder of an international training organization providing online coursework in addiction counseling and recovery coaching. Since 1996, NET Training Institute has encouraged thousands of students worldwide who desire to strengthen families and communities and to serve the wounded, the addicted, the marginalized and the poor. She has also been active in various Christian ministries, filling many relevant roles.

As an author and consultant, she's traveled to 15 nations including Russia, Malaysia, India, Pakistan and Egypt where she's trained Muslim and Christian HIV/AIDS outreach workers for the United Nations. Jean shares with all an uplifting message of hope that the challenges of life can be overcome with grace and courage.

Email: info@netinstitute.org

Website: www.netinstitute.org

Chapter 10

What Happens After Death?

By John Alper

*A Jewish New Ager and follower of Yogananda
discovers the fountain of true life!*

Where many go to retire and die, ironically, is where my life began. I was born in Miami Beach, Florida, in 1951. My young Jewish parents, each the child of wealthy, successful families, sought each other as escape from their controlling families. After five years, my mother became increasingly unhappy and divorced my father. My mother, sister Susan, and I moved to Chevy Chase, Maryland. Not long after, mom remarried a successful young Jewish ophthalmologist—a widower with a daughter about my age.

The two families merged and thus began phase two of the long, emotionally challenging period of my life known as childhood. My new dad was a type A, hard-charging, brilliant doctor. Great bedside manner, but not as great at an intimate father-son relationship. I loved having a new dad, but in many ways, we just didn't mesh.

I was artistic and athletic—a free-spirit dreamer—he was all about medicine—disciplined and controlling. I never felt like I was a first-class son to him. My blood father was more emotionally available and loving, but I was legally adopted and prevented from seeing him after the age of ten. My new father called me a "wild Indian" that he had to tame. He set his sights on that goal, and I guess on some level I appreciated his interest in me, if not his approach. He was a man of excellence and I appreciated that. But inside, I began to rebel against him and some of his values, setting up a conflict and a discontent inside I would hide and struggle with my entire life.

Is that God?

I went to temple the first time when I was about six years old. An impressive sanctuary, it had plush seats, balcony, and two ten-foot-high marble doors (with the Ten Commandments engraved in gold Hebrew lettering) that magically slid apart revealing the gorgeous velvet-draped Torahs within. When the rabbi strode onto the dais, equally impressive with his blue velvet gown and flowing white hair, I whispered to my father, "Is that God"?

I was soon enrolled in Sunday school, graduated to Saturday school, became the president of the temple student council, and had a "standing room only" Bar Mitzvah. The great rabbi called my father not long after and asked if he could meet at our house—he thought I was destined for the rabbinate and wanted to discuss the possibilities.

Such was not my destiny, however. I was not encouraged by my father, who thought I should become a doctor, and I was more interested in girls and sports than studying Torah for the rest of my life.

Besides, there were some unanswered questions that had been bothering me for years—questions about life after death that Judaism failed to address sufficiently. My grandparents all died within several years of each other before I turned 12. Each time we went to temple, I asked the rabbi what happened now that they were dead? Each time, I received a vague response.

Not quite 20 years later, my older sister was killed in a car accident in Washington. I remember the chill that went through me when my father called me in New York that night to tell me the news. I was numb, a hollow feeling. I braced myself against the overwhelming emotion that I knew my family would share and traveled home the next day in a stupor.

Why had this happened? What would become of my sister Susan? Was this it? Was this all there was to life? Where were my grandparents? Once again, why did the rabbi not have a good answer for me?

Other Religions

Over the years, in high school and college, I had been introduced to other religious mindsets. I considered what Buddhism and Hinduism had to say about life and reincarnation. My family was very materialistic and I never saw much happiness in my mother, father, or sisters. There was constant bickering—my mother had everything—looks, money, beautiful home, athletic and artistic prowess—but she was never satisfied. My father was a hard worker, but fought with my mother and was seldom available. My sisters fought with each other and with my parents. I tried to be a peace maker—a diplomat—but I hid my true emotions and led a life behind a mask. I hated the tension. I missed my father in Florida and felt ashamed whenever he called— guilt by association—he was not spoken of highly in our family circle.

So I searched for something meaningful. Something to answer the questions—What was the meaning of life? Why were we here? Was there a way to peace? What happened after death? With no real grounding and looking for escape, it's no wonder I got into hash, pot, beer, and girls.

Transcendental meditation began yet another search for peace and "cosmic truth" while I was in college. I remember the "secret mantra—just for you, John." How exciting! Could there be a special word only for me? I started the practice. For a guy like me, it was not easy to sit still for 5 minutes, let alone 20 minutes. But I tried and got pretty good at it, falling asleep often and waking up kind of refreshed. Nothing dramatic happened, and I remember talking to a friend about how it was going—so-so for him, too, but I found out something; he and I had the same special mantra. That was a little disappointing, but I stayed at it, hoping for revelation. After years, I dropped the practice. I needed something more dramatic.

Those early 1970s were full of excitement, promise of a new culture—free love and high times. I tried it all—sex, alcohol, drugs. I kept searching for something. I just couldn't quite find it.

I moved to Manhattan for grad school—and more girls, a little less pot, more alcohol, and then cocaine. I met a psychic who was a friend of a friend, and I became kind of dependent on her for my sense of security—what would my future be? I found a book of spells once and fooled around with them—trying to get some sense of control over my life! I read Carlos Castaneda—and for a while I was fascinated by shaman witchcraft.

After a few years of working in the film business, I got into advertising and worked for a big New York agency. On one of my many trips to LA, I met a beautiful girl named Sophia, who was a devotee of Paramahansa Yogananda. Next stop, self-realization fellowship (SRF).

Exploring the SRF

Sophia gave me Yogananda's book, *Autobiography of a Yogi*. I read it voraciously. It didn't hurt that she was the most beautiful woman I had ever met, and I would have read the Yellow Pages cover to cover had she asked me to, but the book spoke to me.

This was it! All the answers wrapped up in one book, one philosophy, one man. I was hooked by Yogananda's worldview and the obvious connection he had to the supernatural! Why, his mentor and master, Sri Yukteswar, could transport himself all over the world at will—without an airline—or at least that was the claim that was made. He explained everything. And the girl, well she had the best of both worlds—looks and spirituality.

I tried SRF—I meditated daily. I drank in the philosophy—that my self had all the cosmic things it needed inside to be "fully realized" and that I could find "God." Kriya Yoga, the basis for SRF philosophy, explains in its literature:

> Self-realization is the knowing in all parts of body, mind, and soul that you are now in possession of the kingdom of God; that you do not have to pray that it come to you; that God's omnipresence is your omnipresence; and that all that you need to do is improve your knowing.[1]

Paramahansa Yogananda also said, "The true basis of religion is not belief, but intuitive experience. Intuition is the soul's power of knowing God. To know what religion is really all about, one must know God."[2]

This was heady stuff. It seemed like a good path to peace and spiritual enlightenment. There was a desire to know God, and a seeming path to get there. What was wrong with that?

After a few months back and forth between New York and California, I went to the Visitor Center in LA. I wandered around the grounds, drinking in the good vibes. I visited a sort of chapel that had a line-up of painted portraits hung on the main wall. I stopped to drink in the moment. There was Yogananda, his guru, Swami Sri Yukteswar, Mahavatar Babaji, and the other major yogis of the group, and right in the middle of the mix was a classic portrait of Jesus Christ.

I stared for a while at the paintings, thinking it was a kind of Hall of Fame with a "Last Supper" feel. At that point in my religious understandings, I wasn't sure how Jesus fit in with these men—but there he was among the *yogis*.

Yogananda wrote about "Christ consciousness" and reincarnation. For quite some time, I had thought reincarnation was cool—a great explanation for the "circle of life." I looked around and saw that people lived on different energy levels—at the extremes were criminals who would spend lives in and out of jail or homelessness—low-energy people with lot to learn about how to get on in life. Then there were the more successful people—those who had great jobs, families, positive outlooks. "Saints" like Mother Teresa and "self-realized" *yogis* were at the top of the heap. The low-energy folks would reincarnate at a higher level (hopefully) each time around, and the higher-energy folks got closer and closer to *nirvana*. When they attained it, there would be no more need to cycle through the earthly birth and death routine for another try at perfection.

It seemed like a great explanation for existence. Life either was, or wasn't, cool. But like it or not, life was school. Keep taking courses until you graduate. That explained so much.

I remember being really excited and passionate about Yogananda and his explanation of how life worked. There was enough practical to seem sensible and enough mystery to seem spiritual. But was it truth?

I thought so for years. I kept meditating, waiting for cosmic consciousness to overwhelm me. It made for cool conversation, and my girlfriends liked it. I read Sri Yukteswar's book *The Holy Science*, hoping I could get even deeper and more self-realized. I should say I tried to read his book. It was almost too much and hard to comprehend. (I was an English major with an MBA to boot—I had read plenty of tough stuff in my life, but this was positively Gordian.)

Besides, nothing ever really cool happened. No out-of-body experiences, no flying through lower Manhattan where I lived, no face-to-face with God. I figured I was just not there yet. I wondered a lot what my next life would be. Hopefully, one with more answers and less struggle. I hadn't started yoga postures yet—maybe that was part of the reason I wasn't getting along as much as I had hoped. Who knew? There was a lot that I had to perform in order to achieve oneness with God. It left me feeling vulnerable and unsure whether or not I would ever attain full self-realization—could a Jewish guy from Bethesda, Maryland, become a real *yogi*?

Yogananda explained in one of his books,

The Kriya Yogi mentally directs his life energy to revolve, upward and downward, around the six spinal centers... which correspond to the twelve astral signs of the zodiac, the symbolic Cosmic Man. One-half minute of revolution of energy around the sensitive spinal cord of man effects subtle progress in his evolution; that half-minute of Kriya equals one year of natural spiritual unfoldment.[3]

Wow! I honestly did not know if I had the mental capacity to direct my own life energy. And I became uncertain how many of the other would-be *yogis* could, either.

At one point in my wanderings at the SRF Center, I stopped a devotee wearing distinctive garb denoting her special standing in the organization. I was so excited to be able to ask her some deep, meaningful questions! Was I meditating correctly? Would something special happen soon? And I remember to this day her inability to connect with me—hello, anybody home? No answers, no warmth, really. I needed help, and I felt I was getting the brush-off. I remember a vague sense of fear—of being lost and alienated as I found my way through the grounds to my car. Something was clearly missing here. Where was the love? And once again, too many unanswered questions.

The Next Phase

Not long after the Sophia-phase of my life, I began to get serious with a woman I had known for a number of years through work—a disaffected Catholic looking for love, truth, and a good man. Together, Susan and I began "married life"—zipping out to Santa Fe on our honeymoon, following in the footsteps of Shirley MacLaine! She took us both by surprise—and we thought her view of spirituality was what we had been looking for. It was esoteric, interesting, captivating. But in the end, like all the other New Age philosophies and Eastern religions, for me, unsatisfying.

And then we had our first child. Lucy was the game changer. We settled into domestic bliss for about a month, then we faced the challenges of a colic baby. Not long after that, we had a head-on collision with AIDS—Susan's younger brother became infected and died a pretty gruesome death after six months.

We survived. Barely.

We bought a small house outside the city and left Manhattan. Life in the suburbs was OK. In one of our many deep conversations, Susan and I had made a commitment to never divorce, no matter how bad things got. And things were growing rough between us. She fought depression, and I fought my upbringing and some career choices. I was not the perfectly responsible, bread-winning, chore-doing husband. And Sue was not the happy suburban housewife.

My career was OK, but I struggled for stability. I had gone from producing to directing commercials. It was a whole new ballgame—exciting, adventurous. I was thrust into new levels of artistic challenges I wasn't totally comfortable with. But I relied on my talent and persevered, unwilling to ever give up on what I knew to be my life's work.

I wanted all the good things in life. I had grown up entitled and was now facing how to achieve for myself and my family. Lots of pressure to succeed, and to succeed big! Even though my life-long self-confidence was being challenged, I was still a dreamer.

I wanted the magic of life, but was constantly upended by my short fallings and my wife's growing criticism. We moved from the city to the country. We beautified our house, mowed the lawn. Sue grew flowers. We loved each other in spite of the growing tension. But unhappiness and restlessness hung around me like a dinner guest who wouldn't leave and wouldn't do the dishes, either. I was *still* looking for escape, *still* looking for answers.

When Lucy was about two, we hired our first nanny. Helen called in response to an ad, and after hearing her voice on the phone, I immediately knew she was the one. Sue looked at me flabbergasted when I told her, "She's it. We're hiring Helen." And we did. Helen changed everything. It was through Helen that I met the Lord.

Here was a young Irish-American woman with barely two nickels to her name, a five-year-old daughter, and no husband. But as soon as we met, I saw the joy radiating from her. Not fake, real joy. What a world apart from most everyone else I had ever known!

Over the next six months, we had many discussions when I was home between jobs. She talked about truth and absolutism. I had trafficked in relativism. She talked about God like she knew Him personally. I barely knew myself.

But I was intrigued by this woman with no formal education, who talked about God, Jesus, and the Holy Scriptures, like a college professor. One day, we got into a long conversation about Jesus being the Savior. As a Jew, I had a hard time even saying the name, Jesus. I didn't know much about Him, but had learned somehow that He was forbidden territory.

I found out he was a Jew, *really*, a Jew! And the apostles were Jewish. *Amazing!*

More conversations. Is there truth? Is truth absolute? I was barely hanging on to the false starts with so many paths in the world of relativism. And I still had no answers that truly satisfied.

Two Prayers; Two Answers

One day, Helen asked me if I believed in God. I stumbled in my own thoughts. Yes, I kind of believed in something greater than me, but I didn't know for sure. She said that if I truly sought God, He would show Himself to me. I was intrigued. She said before I went to bed that night, that I should pray and ask God to show me who the "true God" really was. I had a feeling this was something to do with Jesus, but I wasn't sure.

I thought it was some kind of trap to get a Jew to believe in Christ, but I decided to ask God anyway. If there was Truth to be found, I was beyond caring if a man or a myth named Jesus had anything to do with it. The last time I had really prayed to God was when I was four years old. I had a wart on my thumb. My mother told me one night that if I prayed to God really hard and asked Him to take away the wart, He would. The next morning, even though the instructions came from a woman who was not a religious person, that wart was gone.

After 33 years, I prayed my second prayer to God. Helen began bringing some literature and tapes for me to check out. I read books about Christian theology. I was intrigued. I was open. As I read, I began to put some pieces of the puzzle of God and religion and life together. I started to understand the relationship between Judaism and Christianity. It became less about the labels of religion than the truth of God who transcends these labels.

It was a six-month intellectual pursuit. I read books. I read the sinner's prayer. I started to understand things that I never could have embraced before. Now much more than warts disappeared—the veil of darkness began to be removed. I wasn't sold yet, but things were happening.

It's easier to see now looking back. God was doing a work inside me, preparing me for each step of the journey. A number of unusual events occurred for me in that year—one of which was the true turning point in my spiritual search. Susan was invited by a coworker to go to a church near us in Bedford Hills. I had been to some black gospel churches as a boy and Helen had taken us to a very charismatic church in the New York area. Music and soul. Bring it on.

But this church we visited that Sunday was different. We walked in and sat in the back. I looked around at the sea of "wasp" faces and felt kind of uncomfortable. I wanted to leave. No Jews, no gospel music, no thanks.

But as the service began and the music started, I glanced over at Susan, and she looked happy. She had a look of relief on her face, and out of respect for her, I stayed. For some time now, I had been struggling with being a Jew and believing in Jesus. The New Age stuff was clearly not cutting it for me. Judaism had something but was missing the security of the afterlife. And what about the Messiah? Were the Christians right? Had He already come and the Jews were wrong?

I intellectually understood the idea of the Savior, but I could not braid the threads entwining "Christ" (the "Messiah" celebrated by so many Gentiles) and this Jewish guy from Miami Beach.

I listened to the pastor. He had a slight southern accent. He seemed smart, and he was funny. The music was kind of different— a little folky and a few hymns. I was still uncomfortable and a little disappointed. I was kind of hoping I'd found THE place, THE thing, THE final answer to my search. I was hoping that this invitation was going to lead me to the big cosmic solution.

What was with me? I was really having a hard time being surrounded by this sea of white, Christian, non-Jewish faces. I looked out the window. A windy, sunny day. The stark trees were leafless after a long, hard winter.

I checked out the beige handout I had been given when we walked in. Order of service, worship, message, etc. Some names, some announcements of upcoming basketball games. On the back, there was a notice of a special event. That evening, at 7:30, David Mishkin, from Jews for Jesus, presents "Christ in the Passover." Please come.

David Mishkin's presentation ended the last moment I would walk the earth as a New Age, Jewish relativist. His presentation of Jesus in the Passover connected the dots between Judaism and Christianity. He helped erase years of ritual shrouded in mystery and misconception. He opened my mind to the Scriptures, and to the One Helen called "the true God."

Later that evening, I stood near him waiting my turn to ask some questions. We introduced ourselves, and then I remember him asking me if I would like to receive my Messiah that evening. I was scared— what would my parents think? What was my life going to be like? Was this yet another path in my search for truth?

Susan, standing nearby, saw my doubt and nodded her head. "Do it," she was intoning. I turned to David and said, "OK." We prayed. He then asked me to tell a couple people who were sitting back a few rows in the emptying sanctuary. I didn't know what he meant, but I did what he told me. I went back to a guy with a beard and told him I'd just prayed to receive my Messiah. He and his friend's face opened up in a warm beautiful smile. They stood up and embraced me—"Welcome, brother. Praise God! That's the best thing you could have ever done!" A far cry from the robed gal at SRF wishing I hadn't interrupted her walk.

I was beginning to understand that God was a loving, personal Being, independent of me, yet wanting to live inside of me. He had the answers I was looking for. But I needed to ask Him. I needed to come to terms with my imperfections—my unholiness—my "sin." I began to understand that I needed an advocate to help me in this process—that alone, I could not bridge the gap between my imperfect, fallen nature, and a holy God. I needed a Savior.

My New Walk With God

My walk with the Lord has indeed been life-changing. I stopped cursing the day I received the Lord into my heart. Just stopped. I couldn't make those words come out of my mouth.

Sue and I joined a church, started in a small group that we both loved. And Lucy, our beautiful little girl, began Sunday school and listening to praise tapes. Life had drastically, remarkably changed. We began a honeymoon with Christ and Christianity. However, I was terrified of what my parents would think. I didn't know whether I was a Jewish Christian, or a Christian Jew, I had years of labels and cultural stigma to unravel.

I read the Bible. From beginning to end. Days I would stay in my home office room and read and not be able to work. I was compelled to get the whole Scripture into my head. Yet God provided. The Master said, "*Seek first the kingdom of God…and all these things shall be added to you*" (Matt. 6:33). This is true and unfailing.

He saved my marriage. He showed me through His Word, as I sought Him each day, that before I could have my marriage, I had to seek *His* love. I needed to be filled with His love in order to give of His love.

I am in a process now in which I see God in the midst of issues and problems. Through watching Him work in them, in me and in others, I grow in my dependence, reverence, and awe. Time after time in the Bible we see God bringing certain people to the brink and then saving them out of their distress. We see His timing—always perfect. It gives us a sense of awe to witness similar events in our own lives.

Final Thoughts

My journey with the Lord is still very much a work in progress. I entered into relationship with God more through intellectual reasoning than feeling. Mine was not a "leap of faith." God approached me the way He knew I'd respond. This is how He works with everyone. No two individuals are the same, and God knows each and every one of us perfectly—He knows what we need, when we need it, and how to give it to us. We simply need to have hearts that truly seek after Him.

The wonderful thing about God's promise is that relationship with Him, salvation, eternal life, is not dependent on my doing something to gain God's favor. I don't have to jump through hoops or somehow get my aura to line up with my third chakra in order to KNOW that I am a child of God, that my spirit has been reborn, and that the Holy God communes with me. Here is a powerful passage that sums up my story:

> For the word of the cross is foolishness to those who are perishing, but to us who are being saved it is the power of God. For it is written, "I WILL DESTROY THE WISDOM OF THE WISE, AND THE CLEVERNESS OF THE CLEVER I WILL SET ASIDE." Where is the wise man? Where is the scribe? Where is the debater of this age? Has not God made foolish the wisdom of the world? For since in the wisdom of God the world through its wisdom did not come to know God, God was well-pleased through the foolishness of the message preached to save those who believe. For indeed Jews ask for signs and Greeks search for wisdom; But we preach Christ crucified, to Jews a stumbling block and to Gentiles foolishness, But to those

who are the called, both Jews and Greeks, Christ the power of God and the wisdom of God. Because the foolishness of God is wiser than men, and the weakness of God is stronger than men (1 Corinthians 1:18-25 NASB).

One of the great gifts of my faith in the Messiah pertains to life after death. The concept of reincarnation has a lot of holes in it. For instance, where did the first person, or bug, or microscopic protozoa come from—to die, then get reincarnated? What or who runs this process? Who decides whether one "gets to go to the next level" or not? Where do all the people now on earth come from since the world's population has almost always expanded? If souls reincarnate one life at a time, the numbers don't seem to work unless a lot of people come from ants or cows...and (aside from the Scriptures repudiating that) where do the ants and cows come from? The Bible is clear about how many times a person lives:

"...it is appointed for men to die once and after this comes judgment" (Hebrews 9:27 NASB).

The Scriptures are also clear where the rabbi of my youth was vague.

For God so loved the world that He gave His only begotten Son, that whoever believes in Him will not perish but have eternal life (John 3:16 NASB).

For as in Adam all die, so also in Christ all will be made alive. But each in his own order: Christ the first fruits, after that those who are Christ's at His coming, then comes the end, when He hands over the kingdom to the God and Father...The last enemy that will be abolished is death" (1 Corinthians 15: 22-24, 26 NASB).

Yogananda's teaching had some good and peace-seeking elements, and there were references to Jesus Christ and Christ consciousness. But there was so much in conflict with what Jesus called "the Truth." Only one can be right. Settling for a half-truth was not acceptable to me.

In the past, I was floating in a sea of relativism, unsure of my standing with God, and where I would end up after this life, I now have the security of knowing the answer to the question Pontius Pilate asked Jesus (Yeshua) before he delivered Him to be crucified, "*What is truth?*" (John 18:38). Pilate wasn't really looking for an answer, but for those of us who are, Jesus, the (Jewish) Son of God, says, "*I am the way, the truth, and the life*" (John 14:6). There's a world of discovery waiting for anyone who delves into that short sentence alone.

Commentary by Mike Shreve

The main motive behind John's search was a quest for understanding concerning the afterlife. What happens after death? That's what he desperately wanted to know. The "culturally correct" view now is to believe that all religions are basically the same; therefore, all religions lead to the same place. This pluralistic outlook undergirds all New Age teachings. However, when the beliefs of various religions are contrasted just in this subject area, it is impossible for an honest-hearted seeker to arrive at such an illogical conclusion.

Entertain just a few examples. In Buddhism (which does not believe in a soul), the ultimate outcome of a multitude of earthly existences is *nirvana*—a word that means "blowing out" (like the blowing out of a candle). The idea conveyed is cessation of personal existence.

How different is the belief of Hinduism! After many reincarnations, the migrating soul doesn't "cease to be," but instead, arrives finally at *Moksha*—final liberation and absolute, undifferentiated oneness with God. At that stage of spiritual evolution, the soul (*Atman*) actually *becomes* God (*Brahman*)—like the drop of water falling in the ocean—formless and eternal, merging in completely with the omni-presence, omniscience and omnipotence of Ultimate Reality.

Biblically, the view is quite different from both of these. Those who know the Lord will not cease to exist; they will live forever in a *personal* relationship with the Almighty. They will not be formless beings, blending in with some impersonal universal force. Instead, sons and daughters of God will have an actual form. Though utterly one with God, they will still retain a certain measure of individuality. They will have glorified, eternal, heavenly bodies and a perfected personality. They will behold the face of God and worshipfully commune with Him in absolute intimacy. However, God's offspring will never actually *become* God. Neither will they transcend "personhood" into some nebulous, nearly indefinable state of being.

The big issue in all of this is "reincarnation versus resurrection." In Hinduism and New Age spirituality, spirits evolve through thousands of reincarnations until perfection is achieved. In Christianity, there is only one life, and though we will never be able to attain perfection on our own, forgiveness and cleansing are available to us through the cross. The goal is not to rise above all bad karma in order to finally escape some "cycle of rebirths." Instead, we simply receive *"the gift of...eternal life"* by faith in the Messiah (Rom. 6:23). If we die, we are immediately escorted to the highest heaven—for to be *"absent from the body"* is to be *"present with the Lord"* (2 Cor. 5:8) Then on the day of resurrection and redemption, we will be rejoined to our bodies and brought to absolute perfection forevermore. Jesus said:

> *"I am the resurrection and the life. He who believes in Me, though he may die, he shall live"* (John 11:25).

> *"He who believes in Me has everlasting life"* (John 6:47).

What a powerful and remarkable difference!

Endnotes

1. www.ananda.org/ananda/lineage/yogananda.html, a quote of Paramahansa Yogananda, accessed July 28, 2010.

2. www.anandayogaportland.com/SelfRealizationTheOneTruth. htm, a quote from Paramahansa Yogananda, excerpt from the book, Essence of Realization posted online, accessed October 31, 2010

3 Yogananda, Paramahansa, Autobiography of a Yogi (Los Angeles, California: Self-Realization Fellowship, thirteenth edition, 1998) pg. 279.

About the Writer

John Alper is an award-winning director of television commercials and documentary films (APICTURES). He received his BA in English Literature at Williams College, and an MBA in Marketing from Columbia University. He currently lives in Washington, Connecticut, with his wife, Susan, and dog, Fannie. He is blessed with two wonderful children, Lucy and David.

Email: john@apictures.tv

Website: www.apictures.tv

NOW IT'S _YOUR_ TIME!

Thank you so much for setting aside time to read the stories in this book—stories about real people with a real passion for a real encounter with GOD. But now—

It's not about them; it's about YOU!

Are _you_ ready to experience the Lover of your soul, the Great I AM, the LORD of all creation? Certainly it was the Spirit of God who led you to this book and brought you to this pivotal and meaningful moment. You have dwelt on some powerful truth-concepts in the last 234 pages, but now it is time to encounter the Truth-giver Himself.

Knowing about Him pales in significance when compared to actually _knowing Him._

And it's just a prayer away. Really—it's that easy. He made it simple on purpose, so that all can find Him. One Scripture promises that Jesus will "_dwell in your hearts through faith_" (Eph. 3:17). So, as much as you can, fully expect an answer as you invite Him into your heart and life. With as much sincerity as possible, just say a prayer similar to the following:

LORD JESUS, by faith, I invite you into my heart. I pray You will forgive me of any wrongdoings in my past and cleanse me by the precious blood You shed on the cross.

I repent of any idolatry, false worship or wrong spiritual practices and I accept You alone as my Savior and the Lord of my life. I confess that You rose from the dead, and You live forevermore. Because of this, I have the security of knowing that one day, I will be fully changed into Your glorious, eternal image. Thank you JESUS for giving me a spiritual rebirth, a brand new beginning and the "gift of eternal life." I confess that, according to Your Word, we are now in a covenant relationship—forevermore! Amen.

PLEASE CONTACT US!

We really do care about you and want to help you in your search for truth. If you have received Jesus (Yeshua) into your heart and want to know the next steps in this journey of faith—if you need prayer—or if you have questions that still need to be answered, feel free to contact us.

You can write or visit us online:

**SID ROTH
IT'S SUPERNATURAL!**
P.O. Box 1918
Brunswick, GA 31521
(912) 265-2500
www.SidRoth.org

**MIKE SHREVE
THE TRUE LIGHT PROJECT**
P.O. Box 4260
Cleveland, TN 37320
(423) 478-2843
www.shreveministries.org
www.thetruelight.net

In the right hands, This Book will Change Lives!

Most of the people who need this message will not be looking for this book. To change their lives, you need to put a copy of this book in their hands.

> *But others (seeds) fell into good ground, and brought forth fruit, some a hundred-fold, some sixty-fold, some thirty-fold* (Matthew 13:8).

Our ministry is constantly seeking methods to find the good ground, the people who need this anointed message to change their lives. Will you help us reach these people?

> *Remember this—a farmer who plants only a few seeds will get a small crop. But the one who plants generously will get a generous crop* (2 Corinthians 9:6).

EXTEND THIS MINISTRY BY SOWING
3 BOOKS, 5 BOOKS, 10 BOOKS, OR MORE TODAY,
AND BECOME A LIFE CHANGER!

Thank you,

Don Nori Sr., Founder
Destiny Image
Since 1982